HOLY SPIRIT TRAINING

Discover The Predominant Divine Power On Earth

Scott Sanders

sermontobook
.com

Sermon To Book
www.sermontobook.com

Holy Spirit Training / Scott Sanders
ISBN-13: 9780692325063
ISBN-10: 0692325069

I dedicate this book to my mother, Evangelist Christine Sanders, who was the first to encourage me to be sensitive to the Holy Spirit. You put me on the road to developing a thriving relationship with the predominant divine power on earth. Thank you, Mom!

CONTENTS

Who Is The Holy Spirit?

All of us should be moving toward being more sensitive to the Holy Spirit.

I grew up in a denomination that put a lot of emphasis on the Holy Spirit, but only from the perspective of being baptized in or filled with the Holy Spirit with the evidence of speaking in tongues. I always knew this to be an important experience that all believers need, but I had never truly understood who the Holy Spirit was until I sat under Dr. Leroy Thompson's teachings.

For many years of my salvation, I've referred to the Holy Spirit as an "it." As if it were just a thing. And because of that, I never realized the purpose and ministry of the Holy Spirit. Now that I have a fuller grasp on this important topic, I'm able to share my discoveries with you.

In this book, you'll learn who the Holy Spirit really is. And once you begin to embrace the truth about Him, there will be greater manifestation in your life. Let's get training.

The Manifestations of God

In some denominational circles, it would be considered blasphemy to talk about the Holy Spirit, Jesus, and the Father in the same collective context. But that is just bad teaching and bad revelation.

There's a difference between the Holy Spirit being with you and being in you.

It is true that we serve one God, but we must recognize that God has manifested Himself in three predominant manifestations: the Father, the Son, and the Holy Spirit, yet He is still one God. He presented Himself in this way so that we as humans could grasp who He really is. In order to appreciate God's total nature, we must think about Him in these three distinct areas.

Most of the time we ignore the Holy Spirit when we pray. We'll come to the Father in the name of Jesus. We'll even worship Jesus. But we're neglecting the power of the Holy Spirit in our lives.

I know it seems like I'm talking about three different gods, but I'm not. The Father, the Son, and the Holy Spirit are all connected in the mystifying, yet glorious, Godhead. In this book, we're going to discuss the Holy Spirit and how He is central to receiving an overflow of blessings that the Father has set up for those who are in Christ. That's the focus.

And remember, there's a difference between the Holy Spirit being *with* you and being *in* you. He exists in all parts of the earth, but He only dwells inside those who are saved. And through the new birth experience, we have welcomed the Holy Spirit into our hearts, and by doing so, we have become the temple of the living God.

More Than An Experience

There's a big difference between knowing the characteristics of the Holy Spirit and knowing the Holy Spirit as a person.

In the Bible, we see Him as wind, fire, rain, and tongues. In Acts, He is portrayed as a mighty rushing wind on the day of Pentecost. Acts 2:1-4 says, "And when the day of Pentecost was fully come, they were all with one accord in one place. And suddenly there came a sound from Heaven as of a mighty rushing wind, and it filled the whole house where they were sitting. And there appeared unto them cloven tongues like as of fire, and it sat upon each of them. And they were all filled with the Holy Ghost, and began to speak with other tongues, as the Spirit gave them utterance."

There are many spirit-filled, tongue-talking believers who don't know anything about the Holy Spirit. I am not denying that being filled with the Holy Spirit isn't powerful or real—not by a long shot—but the question still remains: Do we truly know the Holy Spirit?

When we lack spiritual understanding about who the Holy Spirit is, we miss out on His ministry and blessings that have been set up for us. So when you address the Holy Spirit, you need to address Him as a person.

This teaching will take some effort to get from your head to your heart, but hopefully by the end of this book, you'll be fully trained in the teachings of the Holy Spirit.

The Last Conversation

Now, this might be a shocker to you, but the Holy Spirit is the predominant divine power on earth right now.

In his last conversation with His disciples, Jesus said, "Nevertheless I tell you the truth; it is expedient for you that I go away: for if I go not away, the Comforter will not come unto you; but if I depart, I will send him unto you," (Saint John 16:7).

Jesus is saying, *I know some of you don't want to see me go but it is better that I leave you physically. So don't worry. The Holy Spirit is going to be in you.*

And when Jesus rose from the grave and ascended to the right hand of the Father, He passed the baton of supernatural operations on earth to the Holy Spirit.

The ministry of the Holy Spirit must be extremely important if Jesus talked about it on one of the last days He was on earth. If you were leaving your family for a long time, I doubt you would waste time talking about the weather or the dirty dishes in the sink. No, you would focus on telling them only the most important information. That's exactly what Jesus did with His disciples.

The Spirit Realm Versus The Natural Realm

There are two different realms, the spirit realm and the natural realm. The spirit realm is where God works. The natural realm is where we live, where God has given us our senses to see, hear, touch, taste, and smell. You have to recognize that God does all His work in the realm of the spirit. God does not do His work in the natural realm. All of your blessings start in the spirit. Your blessings originate in a place that you cannot see. The Holy Spirit is the master of that realm. It is a real place—it exists.

We have to have an unswerving conviction that there are things God has done for us in the spirit realm that we cannot yet see, but we are convicted that it is already there. That is the definition of faith.

Faith is the substance of things hoped for and the evidence, security, and conviction of things not seen. When you are operating in faith, you are saying, "I am convicted of things I cannot see." Well, where are they then? They are in the spirit realm.

There is a difference between going to the bank, hoping there's money in your account, and *knowing* there is money in your account. If you're not sure, you'll swipe your card for a balance. But when you're certain you have money in your account, you'll swipe your card to receive what's there.

Many people have no clue what God has done in the spirit realm. That's why they don't praise Him in the natural realm. Depression comes because you don't even know what God has done for you. This book will teach you to train your senses to know there's more than what the eye can see. You'll learn to say, "Even though I don't see, I know something is there." And you'll be filled with peace when people expect you to fall apart.

But you won't fall apart because you are tapped into the spirit.

For every problem, issue, situation you have, there already exists a prepared blessing that only the Holy Spirit knows.

The Holy Spirit is the master of the spirit realm and all your blessings already exist. What do you need? It already exists. How much do you owe? It already exists. Do you need healing? It already exists. Peace? Already exists.

You must be convicted or you will not take steps of faith to receive your blessing. If you're not convicted that there is money in the bank, you won't go to the bank. But if you know you have money there, you're going to drive to the bank and get what's yours. Your conviction is proven by your actions. We can say a lot of things, but our actions speak louder than words.

The Holy Spirit's job is to discover what the Father has already prepared for those who love Him. He searches the mind of God and says, "I see that for them." When the Father, Son, and Holy Spirit are conversing about what has been prepared for the saints, the Holy Spirit is taking notes.

Ephesians 1:3 says, "Blessed be the God and Father of our Lord Jesus Christ, who hath blessed us with all spiritual blessings in Heavenly places in Christ."

We try to partner with a lot of people that know things in the natural, but have we partnered up with the Holy Spirit?

Some say, "God is going to bless me someday." But the scripture says He already has. Some people interpret that as spiritual blessings, not natural. But in fact, all our natural blessings—everything that is tangible and material—originated in a realm we cannot see: the spirit realm, the invisible realm.

Hebrews 11:3 says, "Through faith we understand that the worlds were framed by the Word of God, so that things which are seen were not made of things which do appear." This verse is a continuation of the definition of faith found in Hebrews 11:1. Everything you can see, hear, and touch was framed by the rhema (spoken word) of God. He spoke it into existence. What you see in the natural was not made by things in the natural. It emerged from an invisible realm into a visible realm. God didn't make the sun out of some physical material. He said, "Let there be light," and there was light.

Our spirit has always existed, long before our physical birthdays. Ephesians 1:4 says, "He chose us in Him before the foundation of the world." I was born on September 2, but I existed in spirit form long before my actual birthday.

No one is in sync with the Holy Spirit one hundred percent of the time. If they were, they would be operating like Jesus, and no one will ever be as perfect as Jesus.

You might be wondering why this is so important. Because all of our blessings are in the spirit realm and in order to receive those blessings, we need to be trained in the Holy Spirit. See, a lot of our blessings are locked up. God didn't lock them up; carnality locked them up. A lack of knowledge is keeping them locked up. But when we get trained, spiritual things will be released that have always been there.

1 Corinthians 2:9-10 says, "But as it is written, 'Eye hath not seen, nor ear heard, neither have entered into the heart of man, the things which God hath prepared for them that love him'. But God hath revealed them unto us by his Spirit: for the Spirit searcheth all things, yea, the deep things of God."

In other words, the Holy Spirit searches the mind of God for us. Why does He do that? So He can tap us on the shoulder and say, "Hey, do you know what the Father has already done for you?"

1 Corinthians 2:11 says, "For what man knoweth the things of a man, save the spirit of man which is in him?

Even so the things of God knoweth no man, but the Spirit of God."

I don't know about you, but I can't read minds. The only way I know what people are thinking is if they tell me verbally. But the Holy Spirit knows what God is thinking and what He has set up for us. He is searching the mind of God and discovering all that He has prepared for those who love Him.

So as you struggle to understand your circumstances in the natural realm, the Holy Spirit has already healed you in the spiritual realm. You're debt free! In the spirit, you're full of peace and joy.

Our Father is a good Father, who has anticipated all our needs and has met each one of them — then He has given us the Holy Spirit, who is the master of the spirit realm to reveal to us what the Father has already done.

1 Corinthians 2:12 says, "Now we have received, not the spirit of the world, but the spirit which is of God; that we might know the things that are freely given to us of God."

Online Banking And The Holy Spirit

Online banking was setup so that you can know in real time what the bank knows. Before online banking, you didn't know what was going on in the bank. Now they give you access into the vault where your stuff is, so you know what's in there. The same thing is true of the Holy Spirit. He's the master of the spirit realm. He's eavesdropping and taking notes in the Heavens and coming to show you what's in the vault.

1 Corinthians 2:10-12 (MSG) says, "But you've seen and heard it because God by his Spirit has brought it all out into the open before you. The Spirit, not content to flit around on the surface, dives into the depths of God, and brings out what God planned all along. Who ever knows what you're thinking and planning except you yourself? The same with God—except that he not only knows what he's thinking, but he lets us in on it. God offers a full report on the gifts of life and salvation that he is giving us. We don't have to rely on the world's guesses and opinions."

There will always be a yoke and a burden. But when you get into rhythm with God, the yoke is easy and the burden is light.

God has a report of all of our stuff, but are we sensitive enough to know what the Father has prepared for us? How can you get depressed if you have the report of all the things that God has prepared for those who love Him? For every problem, issue, situation you have, there already exists a prepared blessing that only the Holy Spirit knows. He knows where the blessing is and when it is supposed to come. He's on earth to share the secrets of the Father, yet we must tap into Him in order to receive them.

We try to partner with a lot of people that know things in the natural, but have we partnered up with the Holy Spirit? God gave you the Holy Spirit to be your partner in this life. Whatever your issue is, you have a partner. And He's not just any partner. He's a supernatural partner who can make anything happen for you at any time.

Dr. Leroy Thompson said, "With the Holy Ghost there is nothing you can't afford." That's powerful! You have a partner that can do anything for you and through you.

The Holy Spirit is Your Life Line

On the game show, "Who Wants to Be a Millionaire," the host asks the contestants questions and when they come to the end of themselves, they'll allow the crowd to give them answers. If they still need help, the contestants are allowed to call a friend. The friend tries to answer the question correctly so the contestant can advance to the next level.

We have a direct line to the Holy Spirit. When we come to the end of ourselves, we can call Him up and say, "I've come to the end of myself. I know you're my partner. Could you help me resolve this?" And He'll tell you exactly what to do. We as believers are struggling because we won't pick up the line because we don't know who He is.

The Sling Shot

Trials are not supposed to be your life. They are a set-up for a comeback. A trial is like a slingshot. You know how with a slingshot, you pull back further and further? It's the same with a trial. The devil is taking you back further and further. But the Holy Spirit says the word—and *boom!*—He launches you into another dimension. Every time I come out of a trial, I don't come out the same way I went in. I come out better.

You Must Cooperate With The Holy Spirit

The Holy Spirit has done some supernatural things in my life. He has spoken to me. He has led me. Even with the paying off of this church building, He told me to do something that was out of the ordinary. He also showed me specific scriptures, and as I was reading them, I knew what I had to do. The Holy Spirit was able to work through me because I cooperated with Him.

We need to be trained in the Holy Spirit. A lot of us are trying to get more education and training in order to land a job and earn more money. But we need to be trained in the Holy Spirit so we can know who He is in the earth and in us.

You must cooperate with the Holy Spirit in order to produce supernatural things. All of your blessings that are locked up in Heaven right now can be released if you simply cooperate with the Holy Spirit. Blessings don't just come without effort on your part. No more than the money in the bank just comes to your house. It's your money, but you have to access it.

Getting In Rhythm With The Holy Spirit

Every time I think about getting in rhythm with the Holy Spirit, it takes me back to when I used to slow dance. I used to dance before I got saved, but I still dance with my wife. Oh yeah, Lady Sanders and I get down. I don't go to parties or clubs and I don't know all the moves, but on a slow dance, I put my arms around my wife and we go to work. She loves it and I love it too. That's a poor marriage that doesn't know how to put a little music on, and I don't put on "Nearer my God to Thee" either.

When you slow dance, someone has to take the lead and someone has to follow. The follower has to relax and let the leader lead. The leader has to know what he's doing. If the follower is going one direction, and the leader is going another direction, it's awkward and uncomfortable. Lady Sanders lets me take the lead. She gets in sync. She doesn't know which way I'm going; she just relaxes in my arms. You have to get in rhythm with the Holy Spirit because you don't know what step He's going to make next.

The Holy Spirit isn't trying to be unpredictable. He's trying to make sure you stay sensitive to Him. The Holy Spirit has a million different ways to deliver your blessings. The question is, "Which one is He going to choose?" While you're anticipating an old way, He has a new way. You don't know what He's going to do next. Many times we think He's going to come the way He came before, but sometimes the Holy Spirit says there's another way. So keep up and stay in sync with Him.

When you anticipate the move, it's bad dancing. Let's say you go right and your partner goes left. Who's going to lead? When we try to make up our own moves, we grieve the Holy Ghost. We must relax and let Him teach us the next step. You cannot anticipate the patterns of the Spirit, because He may move this way one time and that way another time.

There will always be a yoke and a burden. But when you get into rhythm with the Holy Spirit, the yoke is easy and the burden is light.

You don't know which way the wind is going to come and go, you only see the effects. Just like the wind, you must learn to sense the Holy Spirit. You must move with Him.

One thing my mom says to this day is, "You got to be sensitive to the Holy Ghost." That's what I am trying to teach in this book. There is no cookie cutter way to deal with the Holy Spirit. You'll lay hands on someone one time, then God says speak to them the next time.

The Holy Spirit is not trying to confuse you. Whatever your need is, He has a million ways to fulfill it. It's your job to recognize which way He wants to go each time. We must let the Holy Spirit work with us.

But remember, no one is in sync with the Holy Spirit one hundred percent of the time. If they were, they would be operating like Jesus, and no one will ever be as perfect as Jesus. But we do need to increase whatever percent we're at right now. The greater you're in sync with Him, the more you're going to receive blessings from the spirit realm.

Matthew 11:28-30 says, "Come unto me, all ye that labor and are heavy laden, and I will give you rest. Take my yoke upon you, and learn of me; for I am meek and lowly in heart: and ye shall find rest unto your souls. For my yoke is easy, and my burden is light."

There will always be a yoke and a burden. But when you get into rhythm with the Holy Spirit, the yoke is easy and the burden is light.

In the Message Bible Matthew 11:28-30 says, "Are you tired? Worn out? Burned out on religion? Come to me. Get away with me and you'll recover your life. I'll show you how to take a real rest. Walk with me and work with me—watch how I do it. **Learn the unforced rhythms of grace (*emphasis mine*)** I won't lay anything heavy or ill-fitting on you. Keep company with me and you'll learn to live freely and lightly."

Don't force it. Just relax in the arms of the Holy Spirit and let Him lead you. The Holy Spirit wants to produce a fresh plan for you. And remember, not all His methods are alike.

Acts 10:38 says, "How God anointed Jesus of Nazareth with the Holy Ghost and with power: who went about doing good, and healing all that were oppressed of the devil; for God was with him."

Even Jesus partnered with the Holy Spirit. Everything that He did was led by the Holy Spirit. And by observing the life of Jesus, you'll notice that He did not always use the same method. Notice how Jesus, being led by the

Holy Spirit used different methods to receive supernatural provision.

God uses a million different ways to deliver blessings, but we have to be sensitive to the Holy Spirit's leading in order to receive them.

Remember when Jesus turned the water into wine? Mary told Jesus there was no more wine, and Jesus said, "Woman, what do I have to do? It's not my hour." Mary said, "Whatever He tells you—do it." Jesus told them to fill the waterpots and He turned the water to wine. Another time, Jesus and His disciples were asked if they paid taxes. Jesus then instructed Peter to go to the river, look into the mouth of the first fish he caught, and there he would find money to pay the taxes.

Another time, Jesus told His disciples to cast their nets into the water, and they caught so many fish, their nets began to break and their boats began to sink from the weight of the fish.

God uses a million different ways to deliver blessings, but we have to be sensitive to the Holy Spirit's leading in order to receive them. Many are hesitant to live with such reckless abandon, but living in tune with the Holy Spirit causes you to rely on Him all the more.

You won't know how the provision is coming, but you have to go with the leading of the Spirit.

Are you ready to get in rhythm with Him?

CHAPTER ONE

The Role Of The Holy Spirit

By learning how the Holy Spirit functions in your life, you will receive immense spiritual gain. Unfortunately, not every believer longs to be spiritual.

In Romans 8:6, it says, "For to be carnally minded is death; but to be spiritually minded is life and peace." In other words, the opposite of being spiritual is to be carnally-minded, which leads to death in every area of your life.

Wherever you're struggling, the Holy Spirit will grab your hand and expose you to revelation that's going to cause you to break out of that situation.

Saint John 16:12-13 says, "I have yet many things to say unto you, but ye cannot bear them now. Howbeit when he, the Spirit of truth, is come, he will guide you into all truth: for he shall not speak of himself; but whatsoever he shall hear, that shall he speak: and he will shew you things to come."

Jesus is speaking to His disciples. He said, *I have many things to tell you but you don't have the Holy Spirit yet, so you wouldn't even be able to understand what I'm saying.* The Holy Spirit hadn't been given yet. Jesus was not yet glorified (John 7:39).

Once you receive Christ, you can grasp spiritual things. Then, after you get baptized in the Holy Spirit, with the evidence of speaking in tongues, you then rise to another dimension of spiritual sensitivity and sight. John 16:13 says, "Howbeit when he, the Spirit of truth, is come, he will guide you into all truth."

In other words, the Holy Spirit is going to take you by the hand and guide you into revelation that will cause you to be free in areas that currently bind you. Wherever you're struggling, the Holy Spirit will grab your hand and expose you to revelation that's going to cause you to break out of that situation. That truth is going to break the chains that bind you. Events from your past that have haunted you will vanish. You're going to receive truth from the Spirit. He's going to reveal it to you and the chains will break.

How The Holy Spirit Operates

The Holy Spirit will not draw attention to Himself. No self-advertising. Whatever the Holy Spirit hears from the Father, that's what He speaks. The Holy Spirit is in the boardroom in Heaven taking notes. The Father is saying, "I have that set up for Brother Jones."

And when He tells you what He has heard, that's called revelation. It may come through a preacher; it may come while you're reading your Bible; it may come while you're praying.

This book is going to get into how to hear Him, how to follow Him, how to understand His promptings, and how to understand that inner witness.

John 16:13 says, "He will tell whatever He hears from the Father; He will give the message that has been given to Him."

The Holy Spirit's role on the earth is to tell you what the Father has prepared for you and what He wants you to do to receive it.

The Father has relayed the word to the Spirit and the Holy Spirit comes to us and says, "This is what the Father says for you." We better hear what the Father is saying through the Holy Spirit!

The Holy Spirit's role on the earth is to tell you what the Father has prepared for you and what He wants you to do to receive it. If you don't tap into this particular anointing, you're going to miss a lot of revelation. The Holy Spirit is going to show you things to come. That's called vision.

One Bible version says, "He will announce and declare to you the things that are to come, that will happen in the future." In other words, the Holy Spirit says, *You are so important to me and I love you so much that I don't want to keep you in the dark about what I'm about to do.*

Remember when God was about to destroy Sodom and Gomorrah because of their sexually perverted lifestyle? He said, *I'm about to wipe them out, but how can I do this and not tell my friend, Abraham?*

The Holy Ghost wants to make sure you're ready for the next level. He told Abraham, *I'm about to destroy the city, but I just wanted to let you know my plan since we're close.*

The Holy Spirit can give you prophetic messages so that you can prepare for them, be warned of them, make sure you don't do them, or set yourself up so you don't miss what's about to come. He'll give you a "get ready" word.

Luke 2:25 says, "And, behold, there was a man in Jerusalem, whose name was Simeon; and the same man was just and devout, waiting for the consolation of Israel: and the Holy Ghost was upon him."

The consolation of Israel meant the Messiah. Luke 2:26 says, "And it was revealed unto him by the Holy Ghost, that he should not see death before he had seen the Lord's Christ."

The Holy Spirit told him, "*You will not die until you see the Messiah.*" That man was getting older and older, but he was not worried about death because he hadn't seen the Messiah yet.

God will give you a word and that word will keep you alive. He'll say, "You won't die until the manifestation comes to pass." That's why when some of you get sick, you can say with absolute confidence, "I'm not going anywhere. I have a word that hasn't come to pass yet. This sickness is not unto death."

Luke 2:27-29 says, "And he came by the Spirit into the temple: and when the parents brought in the child Jesus, to do for him after the custom of the law, then took him up in his arms, and blessed God, and said, Lord, now lettest thou thy servant depart in peace, according to thy word: For mine eyes have seen thy salvation."

2 Things The Holy Spirit Will Do

The first thing the Holy Spirit is going to do is reveal to you what the Father has said. Secondly, He's going to give you the steps to receive what the Father has said.

The Holy Spirit told Simeon that he wasn't going to die until he saw Christ. Then the Holy Spirit got him up one morning and said, "He's on His way to the temple. Get up and go to the temple right now."

Did you catch that? Simeon was led by the Spirit to the temple and ran right into the promise. His life intersected with destiny, because the Holy Spirit had told him what was about to happen and then gave him the steps to put him there.

The Holy Spirit will tell you things to come, then He will put you at the right place at the right time. Be ready.

CHAPTER TWO

Our Divine Partner

The Holy Spirit is our divine partner. He can make anything happen for us. He wants to work for us, through us, and with us. It is a divine privilege that God would want to partner with mankind.

Psalm 115:16 says, "The Heaven, even the Heavens, are the Lord's: but the earth hath he given to the children of men."

God's domain is in the Heavens and our domain is in the earth. I know people say we're going to Heaven one day, and we are. But Heaven is not the place we'll be for the rest of eternity. If this is news for you, you should study eschatology, which is the study of end times.

You might be thinking, "I've been serving the Lord all this time and now you're telling me I'm not going to Heaven?" I didn't say you weren't going. I said you weren't going there forever.

While the earth endures seven years of tribulation, believers will be in Heaven.

Then, in Revelation it says a new earth is going to come out of Heaven and come back to earth where we will judge the earth with Jesus.

The moment God breathed life into Adam, he became God's partner, and together, they fulfilled God's plan on earth, including naming the animals. God said, "I'll work with you. I'm your partner."

This supernatural power called the Holy Spirit that we cannot see is here to partner with us in order to do great things. It's a wonderful thing to wake up knowing that we have a supernatural partner to guide us through the day.

I know it's tempting to wake up and think, this is *just another day.* But we need to get out of the bed and say, "Holy Spirit, let's manifest some supernatural things today."

God did not save any of us to be ordinary. We have somebody on our side called the Holy Spirit. He's not a god. He is the God. And the Father has presented Him to us as a supernatural partner to fulfill His will on earth.

Another of The Same Kind

As the crucifixion drew near, Jesus knew that his disciples were going to enter a time of mourning. After all, for three and a half years, they were able to see Him, touch Him, and see His miracles nearly every day.

So the night before Jesus was going to be crucified, He told his disciples about the Holy Spirit. He said, *"You're not going to see me anymore. It's best for you that you don't see me, because I'm sending somebody that's not just going to be with you. He's going to be in you. Instead of there being one of me, there are going to be multiples of me all over."*

In Saint John 14:15-16, Jesus says, "If ye love me, keep my commandments. And I will pray the Father, and he shall give you another Comforter, that he may abide with you forever."

There are two Greek words for the word "another": Allos and heteros. Heteros means another sex, but it also means "one of a different kind". Allos means one of the same kind.

Jesus said, *"I'm your comforter right now, but the Father is going to send you one of the same kind."* Jesus, the Holy Spirit, and the Father are one.

John 14:17 says, "Even the Spirit of truth; whom the world cannot receive, because it seeth him not, neither knoweth him: but ye know him; for he dwelleth with you, and shall be in you."

When you get to the end of yourself, you're at the beginning of the Holy Spirit. That's why it's good to get to the end of yourself as fast as possible.

Jesus says, "It's going to be me in another form, but I'm going to be in you. It's going to be the Holy Spirit."

The word comforter comes from the word paraklétos, which means "one that comes alongside to aid". In other words, Jesus is saying, *When I leave you I'm sending you one who's going to come alongside you. He's going to partner with you.*

The Holy Spirit is an intercessor, a strengthener, a securer. He runs to our aid. His purpose on earth is to aid all believers. Can you imagine that? That's why whenever you're taking on something that you feel led by the Holy Spirit to do, you have to believe that you have a supernatural aid working with you.

In the end, we can't take any credit, outside of the fact that we followed His leading. He's the super, we're the natural. What a combination.

It doesn't matter how smart you are. Or how much money you make. Your intelligence can weaken and your money can dwindle. That's when the Holy Spirit steps in and says, "I'll fill in the gap. I'll make up the difference. I'll do what you can't do."

It reminds me of that song: "If you'll take one step, He'll take two." In other words, when you get to the end of yourself, you're at the beginning of the Holy Spirit. That's why it's good to get to the end of yourself as fast as possible.

You might be at the end of yourself right now. If so, you're in a great place. Because that means you're at the beginning of God. And He's called upon your supernatural Comforter to swoop in and rescue you. But you must cooperate with the Holy Spirit in order to manifest supernatural blessings.

You Will Never Go Without

1 Corinthians 2: 9-10 says, "But as it is written, Eye hath not seen, nor ear heard, neither have entered into the heart of man, the things which God hath prepared for them that love him. But God hath revealed them unto us by his Spirit: for the Spirit searcheth all things, yea, the deep things of God."

We must cooperate with Him because He does two things:

1) The Holy Ghost knows everything that the Father has already prepared for you.

2) He gives you the steps and the methods to receive what the Father has prepared.

Every believer knows what I'm talking about when you can just sense that God wants you to do something and you do it. That's called faith. The more you obey the Holy Spirit's prompting, the more you believe in things unseen. Then you begin to set up your life around what you believe—that's called preparation and expectation. The reason you must cooperate with Him is because He will give you the steps. He will tell you what to do to release what the Father has prepared.

People say, "I'm waiting on God." God says, "No, it's waiting on you." Whenever we fail to cooperate with the Holy Spirit, we're going to miss out on the blessing that the Father has set up and we're going to struggle in that area.

Now, I'm not telling you to put pressure on yourself, get mad at yourself, or feel guilty. I'm just saying, recognize you have a partner that's going to show you what the Father has prepared.

Ephesians 1:3 says, "Blessed be the God and Father of our Lord Jesus Christ, who hath blessed us with all spiritual blessings in Heavenly places in Christ."

Notice that the word "blessed" is past tense. He has already blessed you. With how many blessings? All the spiritual blessings in the Heavenly places in Christ. Again, God blesses us in the spirit realm.

So when God blesses us, He does not throw blessings down on earth. He prepares our blessings in the spirit realm, then gives us an arm to reach out and grab. It's called faith.

We see the blessings as they're being revealed by the Holy Spirit, and we take the steps of faith to receive them from the spirit realm.

God anticipates the needs of His people. He's such a good Father. Matthew 6:8 says, "Your Father knoweth what things ye have need of, before ye ask him."

If you're a parent, you know how to meet your children's needs. You buy groceries; you put food in the pantry and the refrigerator. And the kids get up in the morning, expecting to receive something that has already been purchased in anticipation of their hunger. And we're evil compared to our Heavenly Father. If we can lay up provisions for our children, how much more has your Heavenly Father laid up provisions for you?

Every time you have a need, the first thing you should say is, "Lord, I know you have already laid it up. Now,

Holy Spirit, show me where the Father has laid it up, so I can receive what He has already prepared for me." That's how we ought to operate in our lives.

As we stay in sync with whatever God is saying, the Holy Spirit is going to make sure we never go without.

Lose Confidence in Yourself

We must continuously develop our faith and our confidence in the Holy Spirit. You've got to lose confidence in yourself and gain confidence in the Holy Ghost. I was driving the other day and the Holy Spirit said, "Scott, you've learned a lot of things. You have good experience. You're able to do a lot of things." I thought the Holy Spirit was just giving me a compliment. I said, "Yes Lord, I can."

Then He began to show me people who He has done good things through. He said, "What about that person? They may not have the skills or the experience, but when I do it through them, you watch what happens."

Shortly after, a fellow came to me asking for prayer because he wanted to get into business. The first thing that came out of his mouth was, "I don't have a business mind."

I thought to myself, *This is one of those people God was talking about.*

You may not be the sharpest knife in the drawer, but you don't have to be with the Holy Ghost. In fact, He could get more glory out of the dullest knife.

Hear me now. There's nothing wrong with getting educated. I have a Master's degree. But let me tell you, it's the yieldingness to the real teacher, the Holy Ghost, who will show you things to come.

So develop your confidence and your faith in the Holy Spirit. Practice saying, "Holy Spirit, I may not know how to do this, but you do. I'm going to lean on you."

Let Me Work Through You

Remember, Zechariah, the prophet? He was called to prophesy to Zerubbabel to rebuild the temple in Jerusalem.

Now, Zechariah was shown a beautiful vision of a seven-stem candlestick with pipes traveling down to each of the seven stems, and one single bowl over the candlestick, and there were olive trees on each side of the candlestick.

Normally, the priest would come through and keep the wicks clean and the fire burning, but in Zechariah's vision, no one was tending to the candlestick. The trees were feeding oil to the bowl and the bowl was feeding the lamp and the fire kept on burning. The oil represented the Holy Spirit. And God asked Zechariah, "Do you know what this vision means?"

Zechariah 4:4-6 says, "So I answered and spake to the angel that talked with me, saying, 'What are these, my lord?' Then the angel that talked with me answered and said unto me, 'Knowest thou not what these be?' And I said, 'No, my lord'. Then he answered and spake unto me, saying, 'This is the word of the Lord unto Zerubbabel,' saying, 'Not by might, nor by power, but by my spirit, saith the Lord of hosts.'"

He said, *I don't need all your ingenuity, your smarts, I just need you to let me do it through you.* Some people are too gifted. Don't get me wrong, giftedness is good. God gave you gifts, but sometimes your gifts can override the anointing. Your professionalism can take the anointing straight out of something that the Holy Ghost wants to flow through.

For instance, I could preach day and night. I have the gift. Sometimes when you have the gift, you don't rely on the Holy Ghost. There is a powerful lesson in Zechariah's vision. Rely on the Holy Spirit, not on your might and power.

Many times when we force things to happen—instead of relying on the Holy Ghost—we make a mess.

In the Message Bible, Zechariah 4:6 says, "This is God's Message to Zerubbabel: 'You can't force these things. They only come about through my Spirit,' says God-of-the-Angel-Armies. 'So, big mountain, who do you think you are? Next to Zerubbabel you're nothing but a molehill. He'll proceed to set the Cornerstone in place, accompanied by cheers: Yes! Yes! Do it!'"

Many times when we force things to happen—instead of relying on the Holy Ghost—we make a mess. Relax and let God do His thing. He says, "You can't force these things. They only come about through my spirit." That's powerful!

Some people bump their head multiple times and they still don't learn. Give me one bump and I'm ready to say, "Lord, I'm not trying to rely on me. I don't have confidence that I'll make the right decision. Holy Spirit, lead me. If you don't, I'll make a mess of it. I'm relying on you to do through me what I can't do for myself. I know when you get involved, the yoke will be easy and the burden will be light. Holy Spirit, when you get involved there's going to be so much glory to God that everyone will know."

A Wife For Isaac

When God blesses you with abundance, some people might think you're cheating, but let me tell you, when the glory of the Lord is upon you, you know it couldn't be anyone but God. Don't give the praise to man. Give it all to the Lord.

The Holy Spirit is the executor of the Father's estate. He is responsible for taking what belongs to the Father and distributing those blessings to the saints.

In Genesis 24, Abraham is about to die, and he wants to find a wife for Isaac, so he tells his servant to swear to him that Isaac will not take a wife in Canaan, but to go back to his father's house and find a wife for his son Isaac.

The servant's name was Eleazar, which in Hebrew means "helper." Who does he sound like? The Holy Spirit. Abraham instructs Eleazar, "Go and find a wife for my son." Eleazar says, "But what if she doesn't come with me?" Abraham says, "If she does not come with you, then you are released from your oath."

So, Eleazar swears and travels back to Mesopotamia. He brings along ten camels, and says, "Lord, when I ask Isaac's future wife for some water, let her say she'll fetch some water for my camels as well. Then I'll know it's her."

So he goes and finds this beautiful woman standing by the well, and he says, "Fetch me some water." And she says, "Yes, my Lord, and I'll fetch your camels some water as well."

Then Eleazar begins to inquire about the woman's family and discovers that she comes from the lineage of Abraham's brother. He falls on his knees and begins to praise God. He takes out earrings and bracelets and puts them on the woman, as if to say, "I have somebody for you, if you will follow me." She says, "I have to go back to my father's house and explain."

Eleazar talks with the woman's family and her parents consent, saying, "Yes, she can go back with you, but let her stay another ten days."

He says, "No, please, my master is waiting. Let us go now so that I can complete my assignment." The parents ask their daughter, "Rebekah will you go with him now?" And Rebekah agrees.

In a sense, she gets up and follows the Holy Spirit to what the Father had prepared for her. That's exactly how the Holy Spirit works. He'll take you by the hand and guide you right into a prepared manifestation.

When Eleazar found Rebekah, he said, "My master, Abraham, owns all these things and he has a son, and everything that the father owns is the son's. Now it's my job to connect you to the son so that everything the father has worked for can be accessible to you."

Let me tell you something, there are some things that God has in store for you, but they will never manifest without the aid of the Holy Spirit.

Here's the good news: You have a partner to make it happen.

CHAPTER THREE

Picking Up The Signals Of The Holy Spirit, Part 1

What's the best way to comfort someone? You give them encouragement or advice. Words bring comfort. Now, the first thing that you need to understand in terms of picking up the signals of the Holy Spirit is: He speaks. So, when you are filled with anxiety or going through a tough time, the Holy Spirit will speak a word to you and He will comfort you. He's called the Comforter.

Isaiah 50:4 says, "Give me the tongue of the learned that I might speak a word in season to him that is weary."

The Holy Spirit speaks what He hears. So, whatever the Spirit speaks are signals (or messages) from the Father. These are signals that He's projecting from the spirit realm—signals from the Father.

God Wants You To Be Happy

It is wonderful to be saved, but it's even greater to live the abundant life while you're saved. Everybody isn't living the abundant life. A lot of folks are saved but living a struggling life. The way you live an abundant life is to understand and know the ministry of the Holy Spirit.

Saint John 10:10 says, "The thief comes not, but to steal, and to kill, and to destroy: I am come that they might have life, and that they might have it more abundantly."

In the Amplified Bible it says, "The thief comes only in order to steal and kill and destroy. I came that they may have and enjoy life, and have it in abundance (to the full, till it overflows)"

Now that's the kind of life that a saint needs to be living. If you have Jesus, you should be enjoying life in abundance. That's the kind of life we're supposed to be living. You're not going to live that life without understanding the Holy Spirit, being led by the Spirit, having a relationship with the Spirit, or picking up the signals of the Spirit.

The only way you're going to have that kind of life is if you connect with the Holy Spirit. You have to know Him and acknowledge Him. You're going to have to wake up in the morning and say, "Holy Spirit, I know you're here. I know you want to work with me to make supernatural things happen. You're my comforter, my assistant, my strengthener, my paraklétos, my helper. Holy Spirit, I know you speak. And I'm ready to listen."

Do you know that God wants you to be happy? I used to say, "Lord, as long as I have joy, I'm good." I changed that. I'm going to always have joy because it's a fruit of the Spirit. But I want to be happy. God wants you to be happy. See, you can have joy and still not be happy. You can have joy in sorrow but you're not going to be too happy in sorrow. If you're sorrowful all the time, that isn't happiness. But God wants you to be happy.

Learn To Pick Up The Signals Of The Holy Spirit

We must learn to pick up the signals of the Holy Spirit. We must be sensitive to His promptings. The question is where does the Holy Spirit speak? Now, remember that mankind is made up of three parts: spirit, soul, and body. We are spirit creatures first and foremost. In order to really flow with the Holy Ghost, you have to recognize you are a spirit person. You are more spirit than you are physical. You know why I say that? Because your spirit has always existed and will always exist. The Bible says He chose us before the foundations of the world. Now if He chose us before the foundations of the world, we must have existed before the world existed.

We are a spirit that is housed in a body that has a soul. Our body is going back to the dust, but our spirit is going to live somewhere eternally. Before we were born again, our spirit was dead because of sin.

Ephesian 2:1 says, "And you hath he quickened, who were dead in trespasses and sins." When Adam sinned, his spirit died. He did not physically die immediately, but his spirit died. So anybody who was born out of the first Adam is born with a dead spirit, cut off from supernatural and spiritual things. But then when we get born again, our spirit is quickened. That word "quicken" means to be made alive. So, our spirit is made alive when we are born again. "Therefore if any man be in Christ, he is a new creature: old things are passed away; behold, all things are become new" (2 Corinthians 5:17).

Your spirit is one hundred percent brand new. When you are born again, your spirit is recreated and it houses the Holy Spirit. 1 Corinthians 3:16 says, "Know ye not that ye are the temple of God, and that the Spirit of God dwelleth in you?" Where does He dwell? Does He dwell in your flesh? No. Does He dwell in your mind? No. The Holy Spirit dwells in your recreated spirit.

The book of Ezekiel talks about the spirit a lot. Ezekiel 11:19 and 36:26 says, "A new heart also will I give you, and a new spirit will I put within you: and I will take away the stony heart out of your flesh, and I will give you an heart of flesh."

The Holy Spirit does not speak in the air somewhere. He speaks on the inside of you. He speaks to your spirit. Whatever He hears, He speaks to your spirit.

Now we're back in the place where Adam was in the Garden in the cool of the day having fellowship with God. God can talk to us, but He speaks to us in our spirit. Even when you hear a rhema, it may come through your ear and go through your mind, but it's your spirit that says, "Amen."

When the Holy Spirit receives a message from the mind of God He begins to work with you to manifest what He heard. The Holy Spirit then passes God's message on to your spirit and then your spirit will speak to your mind. That's called an inner-witness. He'll speak in a still, small voice.

If you want guidance, you're going to have to mind your spirit. The spirit sends signals, but if you're minding your circumstances instead of picking up the signals from your spirit, you're going to think you're poor when actually you're rich.

Now, if I'm leaning on my mind and my flesh, what would you call me? Carnal, of the senses, leaning on what I can see, hear, touch, taste, and smell. A lot of Christians live like that. If you're carnal, the Spirit may be talking to you, but you're not sensitive to what He projects because you're dependent on only what you can hear with your natural ear.

When you have the Holy Spirit housed inside you, you are whole. You might say, "I'm going to get better one of these days." But in reality, there's a part of you that can't get better. Your spirit is already one hundred percent complete. If you told somebody you were perfect, you wouldn't be lying. Just tell them a third part of you is. Your spirit which has been created in righteousness and true holiness is perfect and cannot be improved upon. (Ephesians 4:24).

Now when my spirit sends a signal to my mind and I begin to understand it, that's called revelation. Your recreated spirit is the candle of the Lord.

Proverbs 20:27 says, "The spirit of man is the candle of the Lord, searching all the inward parts of the belly." What do you do with a candle? You light it. What do you use a candle for? To see. What did they use it for in those old days? For light. What does it say about the word in Psalms? "Thy word is a lamp unto my feet, and a light unto my path."

Light is for guidance, illumination, and revelation. The spirit of man is the candle. That's where the Holy Spirit brings light into man. Your spirit is lit up with revelation. He's trying to get that light to your mind.

The Lord enlightens us and guides us through our recreated spirits.

If you want guidance, you're going to have to mind your spirit. The spirit sends signals, but if you're minding your circumstances instead of picking up the signals from your spirit, you're going to think you're poor when actually you're rich.

Our born again spirit is powerful. That's why it's so important to figure out how to pick up its signals, because a lot of times we don't pick up the signals. If you're sad, mad, depressed, oppressed, or stressed, you aren't picking up the signals. Your spirit is screaming at you; all is well, but you can't pick up the signal.

Peter would call this the hidden man of the heart, (1 Peter 1:4). Your spirit knows things that your head doesn't know because the Holy Spirit is in your spirit.

Your mind has to catch up with what your spirit knows. You know in the old days, you had the analog radio in the car, and in order to get the station you had to turn that little knob, and you'd try to get that thing right where it needed to be so you could pick up signals. That thing was called a tuner. Even in your car right now it'll say, "Tune." We have to learn how to tune in. We have to learn how to tune in to the Holy Ghost and how to tune in to our own spirit.

When you start picking up signals from the spirit, there will be some preparation. If you're not preparing for anything right now, you haven't heard anything from the Holy Ghost.

When you really pick up the signal from the Spirit, you may not know everything that's going on, but you're sitting there like, "Oh my God, something big is happening. Oh God, I'm sensing something." It's called spiritual perception. We must walk by faith and not by sight. If you walk by sight, you're carnal. But is faith sight? No. Faith is not sight. Faith is real seeing, but it is not physical sight.

Hebrews 11:1 says, "Now faith is the substance of things hoped for, the evidence of things not seen." So when you're dealing with faith, you're dealing with things you can't even see. But when you really know it's real, no one can convince you otherwise.

When you start picking up signals from the spirit, there will be some preparation. If you're not preparing for anything right now, you haven't heard anything from the Holy Ghost. You have to be looking forward to something. That's how you live to be one hundred and twenty, because you have something to look forward to.

1 John 2:20 says, "But ye have an unction from the Holy One, and ye know all things." Your spirit that houses the Holy Spirit knows all things. The Lord enlightens us and guides us through our spirit. We have to become spirit-conscious. Again, that's minding the spirit.

When David Became King

There were three kinds of people in the Old Testament who were anointed by the Spirit: prophets, priests, and kings. The Holy Spirit would begin to reveal things to them.

When you begin to flow with the Holy Ghost, He may not tell you all the details. He may just give you step one and you won't receive step two until you complete step one by faith.

Remember when Samuel was crying because God had rejected Saul as king? Samuel was interceding for Saul, begging and saying, "Lord take him back." And God said, "How long are you going to be down here crying for this man? I have rejected him. Get your oil and go to Jesse's house and anoint the king."

So Samuel went to Jesse's house with the cruse of oil. When he arrived, he said, "Jesse, I come here to anoint one of your sons." It would have been easy if Jesse only had one son, but he had eight. To make it more difficult, God didn't specify which son would be king.

They had to bring one son after the other. Samuel would look at each son and say, "Oh, he looks like a king, tall and strong looking. He must be the king." But the Holy Spirit would say, "He isn't the one."

1 Samuel 16:7 says, "But the Lord said unto Samuel, Look not on his countenance, or on the height of his stature; because I have refused him: for the Lord seeth not as man seeth; for man looketh on the outward appearance, but the Lord looketh on the heart."

In other words, don't try to follow your eyes; follow the spirit. Your eyes will get you in trouble. Your eyes will make you pick the wrong person.

Samuel went through seven of the sons, but none were to be king. He must've been in the Spirit because most of us would have said, "Who's the best looking one? Eenie, meenie, miney, mo…"

But what did Samuel do? He said, "The Holy Spirit is not witnessing to me on any of these. Do you have another son?"

Jesse replied, "Oh, I forgot all about David. He's my youngest. He's out there with the sheep. I'll go get him."

When David came in, smelling like the animals, The Holy Spirit said, "He's the one." Samuel poured the oil on that boy in the midst of his brethren and anointed him king.

Elisha's Prayer for Rain

When Elisha needed rain, he said, "Bring me a minstrel." When I'm preparing for my Bible classes and sermons, I have worship music playing and I sing. It may bring tears to my eyes, but when that music is playing, my spirit is open. I'm no singer, but I'm a worshipper.

Elisha knew how to get in the presence of the Lord. The minstrel began to play and the Spirit began to speak to him, saying, "You will not see wind nor rain, yet this valley shall be full of water."

Elisha picked up the signal of what the Father's will was. This is all we need to do.

Elisha said, "The rain is coming." That's revelation. Then he said, "Dig ditches." That's preparation. He said, "If you want to get this manifestation, first of all, it's coming. Secondly, get ready."

And they dug. They probably dug all night. They got up in the morning and the water began flowing, and there was no rain from the sky but there was a flood in another city—miles away—in a higher elevation. It flooded so much that the water came down to the valley. Everybody that had a ditch got some water.

You have to know how to flow with the Spirit. And He will speak to you.

CHAPTER FOUR

Picking Up The Signals Of The Holy Spirit, Part 2

When I was in college, I got a Master's Degree in Tele-communications. Telecommunications is communication at a distance. Phone companies have switches that communicate to one another, either through wire or microwave signals. They communicate from one city to another.

When the Holy Spirit is speaking to you, He's in you, but He's picking up signals from God.

There's a network in the Heavenly realm. It starts with the Father. He is speaking and then He sends a message to the Holy Spirit. The Holy Spirit then sends it to our spirit. Our spirit then sends it to our mind. Then we begin to get manifestation. It's called a Supernatural Network.

But if any node on the network is down and inoperable, it cuts off the signal. It'll "drop the call." We don't want to drop a message from the Holy Spirit. That's why we've got to learn how to pick up the Holy Spirit's signals because our spirit, which houses the Holy Spirit, knows things that our mind doesn't know.

5 Ways to Pick Up the Signals from the Holy Spirit

1) You must position yourself to pick up the signal

Again, remember the radio tuner in those old cars. You had to turn the knob and you would hear all those noises until you got to the station you were looking for—only then could you hear clearly. That's called positioning. Likewise, we must position ourselves to pick up the signals of the Holy Spirit.

One of the ways to position yourself to pick up the Holy Spirit's signals is through praying, fasting, attending church services, and exposing yourself to the Word of God.

In 2 Chronicles 20, Jehoshaphat was up against three kings and hundreds of thousands of people coming up against Judah. He prayed and sought the Lord. Then the Spirit moved upon Jahaziel, the son of Asaph, and Jahaziel began to prophesy, saying, "You will not need to fight in this battle, because this battle is not yours—it's the Lord's."

The first thing Jehoshaphat did was fast and pray. This positioned him to be open to the signals of the Spirit and follow the instructions to win the battle.

Not only did Jehoshapat fast and pray, but he became open to the prophetic word the was spoken by another man. 2 Chronicles 20:20 says, "And they rose early in the morning, and went forth into the wilderness of Tekoa: and as they went forth, Jehoshaphat stood and said, 'Hear me, O Judah, and ye inhabitants of Jerusalem; Believe in the Lord your God, so shall ye be established; believe his prophets, so shall ye prosper.'" Many people say, "I only hear from God", but notice that Jehoshaphat said, "believe in the Lord your God, but also believe his prophets." When you're really open to the Holy Spirit, you'll be open to the message that He sends through others.

2) **You must mind the spirit**

As humans, we are a triconomy, a three-part being: spirit, soul, and body. As you think in your mind, so is your life. Your life is nothing but a compilation of thoughts over time. Wherever you are in your life, your thoughts got you there, whether positive or negative. If you're in a negative place, all you have to do is have a change of mind and you can break out of a negative place into a positive one.

In your born again spirit, the Holy Ghost seals you. The Holy Spirit resides on the inside of the spirit, not the mind, not the body. The Holy Spirit is taking His residency in the spirit, so your spirit knows all things (1 John 2:20).

When your mind is more concerned with what you can see, hear, touch, taste, and smell, you can't pick up the signals from the Spirit.

Romans 8:6 says, "For to be carnally minded is death; but to be spiritually minded is life and peace." So if you're minding the spirit, you'll experience nothing but life and peace. But if you're carnally minded, every misery that is derived from sin will hit your life. You're saved, but you're not minding your spirit .

When you're minding the spirit, the spirit will know more than your head, but it's always sending signals, so your mind is catching up with what your spirit knows. Every now and then when it picks up a signal from your spirit, it begins to believe; it begins to expect; it begins to imagine.

You can't have manifestation without imagination. You must see yourself there before you ever get there. The Spirit will begin to tell you things and show you things that already exist in the spirit realm.

You must have confidence that your spirit knows what your mind doesn't know. Have you ever gotten to a place where you don't know what to do? Guess what? That's an infirmity God says we will have, but He also said we have a helper called the Holy Spirit. So, you have to look to your spirit first for direction, instruction, and knowledge.

When you don't know what to do, you've got to become so spirit conscious that you say, "What is my spirit saying?" Not what people are saying, not what my circumstances are saying.

There are a lot of voices out there. But there is the voice of the born-again recreated spirit. I don't know if it's called a conscience or intuition, but you will hear your spirit begin to convict you. That's the Holy Spirit giving your spirit a signal and your spirit telling your mind how to live.

3) Stay full of the Spirit

Ephesians 5:15-16 says, "See then that ye walk circumspectly, not as fools, but as wise, redeeming the time, because the days are evil."

That word "redeem" means to buy back the time. It means to take advantage of every opportunity. There are going to be some opportunities that God gives you, and you need to be sensitive to the Holy Spirit to take advantage of them. But He said you have to walk circumspectly. The word "circumspect" means to circle; it means to move around; it means to be cautious; it means to make sure you're aware.

Ephesians 5:17 says, "Wherefore be ye not unwise, but understanding what the will of the Lord is." Of course we all want to know what the will of the Lord is, but let me show you how it's going to work. Verse 18 says, "And be not drunk with wine, wherein is excess; but be filled with the Spirit."

When you receive the Baptism of the Holy Spirit, you will hear yourself speak in a language that you were not taught. That's being filled with the Holy Ghost or baptized in the Holy Ghost.

Many of us have had the experience of being baptized in the Holy Spirit or we've had that one encounter with the Holy Spirit. We did not speak in tongues yet, but we felt the fullness.

One way to stay full is to sing to yourself. I don't care if you can't carry a note. It's beautiful to God.

A young man came by my office recently when I was rather busy, but I sensed the Holy Spirit wanted me to listen to him. He wanted me to lay hands on him, but it surprised me because I had talked with him before about the baptism of the Holy Spirit and I found out that he was from a Baptist background. He said sometimes that denomination kept him from opening up, but he did have an encounter where the Holy Spirit flooded him. He just didn't speak it out and speak in his heavenly language. But that day he received the Baptism of the Holy Spirit, because when I anointed him with oil and laid my hands upon him, I began to confer the blessing and speak a word of knowledge and a word of wisdom over his life and he began to flow beautifully, like he had been speaking in tongues a long time. He said, "I held back because I was Baptist." There's nothing wrong with being a Baptist—or Lutheran, or Catholic, for that matter—just so long as you're filled with the Holy Ghost.

Another way you stay full of the Spirit is by, "Speaking to yourself in psalms and hymns and spiritual songs," (Ephesians 5:19). The Amplified Bible says, "…offering praise with voices and instruments and making melody with all your heart to the Lord."

Did you know the book of Psalms is nothing but one hundred and fifty songs? The word psalm means song. David wrote these psalms while he was in some of the most difficult times of his life. He was keeping himself full or sensitive to the Holy Spirit. God was giving him these songs.

One way to stay full is to sing to yourself. I don't care if you can't carry a note. It's beautiful to God. Another way of staying full of the Spirit is giving thanks always for all things unto God. People who complain can't hear the Spirit. But a thankful heart is a sensitive heart to what the Spirit is saying.

When you stay thankful, you stay full; you stay sensitive; you begin to pick up the signals from the Holy Spirit.

Some people are not very appreciative. They are spoiled. Look at everything God is doing for you right now. You might not have the job you want, but be thankful that you have one. You might not have the house you want, but at least you have a roof over your head. Thank Jesus for that.

Also, submission keeps you sensitive to the Spirit. Ephesians 5:21 says, "Submitting yourselves one to another in the fear of God." Submitting yourself to God's order in the church is the same as submitting yourself to Christ.

If you don't submit yourself to anybody, you can't hear the Holy Ghost. I hear people say, "I don't have to be under this person or that person. God speaks to me."

It doesn't work that way. You have to submit yourselves. Submission is key to hearing. If you can't submit yourself to the church, you cannot hear the Holy Spirit. Staying full of the Spirit is all about submitting.

4) Praying in tongues

One of the things that is going to enable you to pick up the signals from the Holy Spirit is to pray in tongues on a regular basis.

In my private life I speak in tongues probably more than most people. I do it all the time. I get up in the morning praying in the spirit. I'll be at the store and I'll be praying in the Holy Ghost. It isn't out loud. Nobody hears me. It will be in hushed tones. If you were to hear it, it would sound like a mumble. I pray in the spirit while I'm preparing my messages. When I'm preparing my messages, I pray in tongues so that the Holy Spirit can tell me what to talk about, even what to teach. Many things in this book have come from the Holy Spirit dropping it into my spirit.

As I'm praying in the spirit He sends a signal. I pick it up in my mind because my mind begins to be more sensitive to the Holy Spirit as I pray in tongues.

Some people don't want to be filled with the Holy Ghost with the evidence of speaking in tongues, but you don't know you're missing the biggest part of your salvation. You can't even operate with the Holy Ghost if you don't have that experience and then pray in the Holy Ghost on a regular basis.

When you are filled with the Holy Ghost with the evidence of speaking in tongues, you receive a prayer language and you can pray in tongues anytime. Maybe you tried it and it didn't work. Well, try again! I don't care if you get two syllables: Ecah, Ecah, Ecah. After a while you'll pick up a third syllable: Ecah-Ba. That might not sound like much, but your spirit is working. Ecah-Ba!

In 1 Corinthians 14, Paul was teaching the Corinthian church how to properly operate in the gift of tongues.

1 Corinthians 14:4 says, "For if I pray in an unknown tongue, my spirit prayeth, but my understanding is unfruitful."

You may not understand everything, but that's okay. Let your spirit do what it needs to do.

When you're praying in tongues, your mind goes inactive. Scientists did a study where they put the electrodes on somebody's brain to pick up the signals when they began to speak in tongues and there was no signal because the brain doesn't even know what's happening. Your brain says, "I will allow the spirit to do what it needs to do even though I don't understand."

You may not understand everything, but that's okay. Let your spirit do what it needs to do. A lot of times, people don't pray in tongues because it doesn't make sense to them, but this is not about sense. It's about power and revelation. Who cares if it makes sense to your mind? When you pray in an unknown tongue, your spirit is praying.

Paul had greater revelation than any apostle. Peter walked with Jesus, but didn't have the same revelation that Paul had. In fact, Peter said in his Epistle, "Paul said some things that the unlearned and unstable wrestle with, but it is scripture". Paul's secret to his revelation is found in 1 Corinthians 14:18, when he says, "I thank my God, I speak with tongues more than ye all."

Why was he thanking God? Because he knew that as he prayed in the spirit he was going to pick up the signals of the Holy Ghost and manifest supernatural things. Paul, the man who wrote most of the New Testament, is saying it is great to pray in tongues.

1 Corinthians 14:2 says, "For he that speaketh in an unknown tongue speaketh not unto men, but unto God: for no man understandeth him; howbeit in the spirit he speaketh mysteries." So when you begin to pray in tongues, you are speaking mysteries. A mystery means something that's covered, but speaking in tongues is going to uncover the mystery.

1 Corinthians 14:13 says, "Wherefore let him that speaketh in an unknown tongue pray that he may interpret."

So while you're praying in tongues, you can either ask God for interpretation or say, "I know you're going to reveal this to my mind."

Then the Holy Spirit will bear witness to your spirit and you'll begin to be led by the Spirit. The Holy Spirit will drop things into your spirit and then your mind will pick up the signal. But it would not have picked it up if you had not prayed in the spirit. Because praying in the spirit is the greatest way to pick up the signals of the Holy Spirit.

Our Unpaid Debt

Several years ago, my wife and I had close to twenty thousand dollars of unpaid debt. And I told her one night, "I'm tired of paying these bills. We're going to put together a two-year plan and get out of this twenty thousand dollar debt."

My wife agreed with me and we had a prayer of agreement right on the side of our bed. I said, "In the Name of Jesus, Father, I just know that you're going to help us get out of this debt. We agree right now that this debt is taken care of, and we're going to be out of debt." It was a two-minute power prayer and we went to bed.

Then, while I was praying in the Holy Ghost one morning, the Holy Spirit said, "Your taxes are wrong." So I called some friends and said, "Who do you use for taxes?" And they gave me some recommendations and I took the current year taxes to another accountant and he said, "Well, Pastor Sanders, it is four thousand dollars." I said, "My goodness, I have to pay four thousand dollars!" He said, "No, no. That's your refund." I said, "Wait, Brother! You aren't sending me to jail now. Did you cheat? What did you do? We always pay taxes."

He said, "No, " Then he said, "Let me take a look at your older taxes. You can go back three years and redo them."

So, he redid our taxes, and pretty soon, checks started coming in like clockwork. Bang—four thousand dollars, two thousand dollars, fifteen hundred dollars. They just kept coming. Every time they came in, I would pay the debts until all our debt was gone. This miracle didn't happen in two years, like my wife and I had agreed upon. It only took four months. And the money was there all along. I just needed to ask the Holy Spirit for help.

CHAPTER FIVE

Picking Up Signals Through Meditation

Meditation is a master key of the Holy Spirit. We miss so much when we don't meditate. Meditation is something you do after you've heard or after you've read. The word "meditate" means to go over something in your mind, to turn it over, to let it sink in.

You will begin to hear what the Holy Spirit is saying clearer when you meditate. See, the devil doesn't care what you get when we're at church. He just doesn't want you to work it when you get home. He doesn't even care about you getting healed in church. He just wants to make sure you don't keep it when you leave. It's going to be through meditation that it gets from your head to your heart.

Meditation is not memorization. A lot of people can quote scripture but it's not in their heart. I have learned scriptures over the years, but that's not meditation. You need to memorize it to meditate, but memorization is not necessarily meditation. There are a lot of people who can quote scripture, but they have no proof to say they've been meditating at all, because meditation is going to bring manifestation.

> *The more you're in the Word, the more you can pick up the signals of the Holy Spirit.*

You are not working with the Holy Spirit if you're not meditating on the Word. You may have been baptized in the Holy Ghost, but you are not working with the Holy Spirit. You might be saved—good—but you're not really working with Him until the Word gets involved. Because when the Holy Spirit speaks, He speaks in Bible language. So the more you're in the Word, the more you can pick up His signals.

Most every time God directs me to do something, I've got to get that Word and I begin to meditate on it, then out of my meditation He shows me what to do. He gives me the application of it.

When we paid off our church building, I began to work a word in my heart about this woman who was in debt in 2 Kings 4. She came to Elisha and said, "My husband served you, and now the creditors have come to take my two sons away. What are you going to do for us?"

Elisha said, "What do you have in the house?"

She said, "A little oil."

He said, "Go and borrow some vessels, and when you go into your house, close the door and pour it into those vessels."

I began to meditate on that scripture. As I began to go over the Word, God began to say, "I'm going to show you how to get out of debt." I wasn't thinking about getting out of debt in the church, but as soon as I began to meditate on that scripture, the Spirit began to say, "I want you out of debt, and I want you to use this scripture to get out."

I didn't know how, but I knew God was going to use that scripture to get us out of debt. So what did I do? I kept on meditating. I kept on reading that passage, and I'd preach it every now and then.

Then God began to tell me, "Now what I want to show you is that what she had in the house was less than what the vessels could hold, yet when she poured her oil into those big vessels, they were full. She kept on pouring into bigger vessels and they were getting full from a small vessel. Now, that small vessel is your account, and the big vessel is the mortgage. I want you to pour into that mortgage."

Meditation means going over and over the Word of God until you pick up the signal.

How did I get that? By meditating. I don't just use that scripture for one encounter. Now it's my revelation and I can use it anytime if I have too limited resources to put in something big. I can use the same thing I've been meditating on and, if it worked then, I have the revelation and it'll work easier the next time.

Meditation is going to give you the revelation and then it's going to give you the application of how to do it. God said, "Start sending money to the mortgage." I said, "We don't even have that much money to send." Then God told me, "To the extent that you send, that's what I'll send back to you. If you pour out a little, I'll replace a little. If you pour out a lot, I'll replace a lot." I was like, "Lord, that don't make no sense."

But I began testing it. Folks at church started getting on board too. And the money began to flow. I saw it with my own eyes. I would put out ten thousand dollars and the next Sunday, boom, a big offering would come in. I would say, "Wow! Where did that money come from?" And God said, "I told you the more you pour out, the more I'll pour in." And He kept His promise and made it happen. The money just kept flowing in.

Meditation means going over and over the Word of God until you pick up the signal.

Some people want to read a whole bunch of chapters and that's okay. Reading is good, but meditation is key. Meditation is going over the same word until you pick up the signal from the Spirit..

Meditate Anywhere And Everywhere

When I started pastoring my church in 2003, I would fast almost every day of the week. And then Saturday I'd study all day. Now, eleven years later, on Saturday nights I'm in my room with my wife. She hardly sees me crack open a Bible. But I'm meditating all day. I'll be watching the game and shouting, "Good shot!" Meanwhile, I'll be going over the Word in my mind.

I'm more anointed now than I was then. Because even though I was praying and fasting more back then, meditation does more than prayer and fasting. Do you need to pray and fast? Yes, but meditation helps you pick up the signals quicker and it's more intense than just sitting around all day.

I decided several years ago that I'm not sitting around all day on Saturday. When I'm out doing errands, I'm going over scripture in my head and the Holy Spirit is showing me truth. I'm not stressed out; I'm meditating and I'm getting more.

When you begin to meditate on the Word, you draw life out of the Word. And the Holy Ghost begins to talk to you. Your spirit begins to hit your mind and your mind begins to say, "I see it now."

Sometimes I get up in the morning and He'll put a scripture on my mind and He wants me to go to that scripture and work on it. Other times, the Holy Ghost will say, "I got a whole bunch to say to you, so just sit down."

So when you get up in the morning to pray, you have to let Him do what He wants to do. My whole prayer life changed. I use to say, "Lord, I'm not saying enough, I'm not saying enough." But then I heard Him say, "I don't want you to say something every day. Sometimes I just want you to sit in my presence and learn to wait on me."

Some mornings I put some music on and just listen, and the Holy Spirit begins to fill me, and I begin to sing.

In meditation your spirit is put in charge and your soul begins to obey your spirit.

When you are born again and you begin to meditate in the Word, your spirit is back in charge, because your spirit now has to influence the soul.

If your mind is not convinced that there is something greater from the spirit, it'll always be following the senses and you'll struggle. But through meditation, your soul starts hearing the Word, and saying, "I trust."

Meditating in the Word renews and trains the mind or the soul. When you meditate on the Word, you're actually training your mind that there's more to life than what the eye can see.

The devil doesn't want anybody to see the glory of God on you. That's why he keeps you busy with issues.

Romans 12:1-2 says, "I beseech you therefore, brethren, by the mercies of God, that ye present your bodies a living sacrifice, holy, acceptable unto God, which is your reasonable service. And be not conformed to this world: but be ye transformed by the renewing of your mind, that ye may prove what is that good, and acceptable, and perfect, will of God."

You've got to have your mind re-programmed. Through meditation the Word reprograms your mind. The Word begins to tell your mind, "You have more than enough." The Word begins to tell your mind that, "The supply is greater than the demand." The Word begins to tell your mind, "By His stripes you were healed over two thousand years ago."

When you begin to meditate on the Word, the power of the Word is going to hit your body and hit your life because as you think, so will you be.

As you're meditating on the Word, it's changing your ideals. It's changing how you feel about yourself. There's no way you can meditate on the Word and have low self-esteem.

I tell people all the time that I could write a book on low self-esteem. And they say, "But you talk so great about yourself all the time." Well, I've been meditating on the Word for a long time. I went through every school of low self-esteem and graduated. The more you recognize who you are, the more the devil is scared. He doesn't want you to think about how powerful you are in Christ. He's going to throw all kinds of things at you so you won't think about what the Words says. He doesn't want it to get in your heart because he knows if it gets in your heart, it will get in your life.

When it gets in your life, everybody is going to see the glory of God. The devil doesn't want anybody to see the glory of God on you. That's why he keeps you busy with issues. We have a lot of busy people in the church. Busy doing nothing. If only we would rely on the Holy Ghost instead.

When you begin to meditate on the Word, you are going to receive a rhema word—a specific, personal, time-bound word that will release power into your life. Rhema comes through meditation. It comes by hearing the Word of God.

Without the Holy Spirit, we all have an ignorant and insensitive soul. But when you start to meditate on the Word, your intellect begins to understand spiritual things, and that's called illumination. It's like the light comes on.

There are five parts to the human soul: memory, intellect, imagination, emotions, and will. When you begin to meditate on the Word, God begins to bring other scriptures to the surface of your memory. He told His disciples, "When the spirit of truth comes, when the Comforter comes, He's going to bring all things back to your remembrance" (John 14:26).

Without the Holy Spirit, we all have an ignorant and insensitive soul. But when you start to meditate on the Word, your intellect begins to understand spiritual things, and that's called illumination. It's like the light comes on. Meditation will work on the intellect.

Then meditation will begin to work on your imagination. You use your imagination for everything. Out of your imagination comes faith, fear, disbelief, and doubt. Your imagination is made up of images. You have to see it before you can be it, and when you begin to meditate on the Word, you begin to see yourself prospering and succeeding.

Through meditation, the Holy Spirit will begin to give you pictures because you can only go where you see. A lot of people never go anywhere because they can't see beyond where they are. The devil will have you looking so much at your present situation that you cannot see your future.

Your imagination is like a television. It'll put the reel in and show you where you're going. It'll show you things to come. When the Holy Spirit starts working with you, you begin to see yourself in a whole different light. You begin seeing yourself do things that you never thought you could ever do.

For me, I saw myself speaking to people. I began to imagine that I was a preacher. I began to record myself. I began to hear myself on the recorder and I couldn't believe what I was hearing. That's when I realized I had a gift for preaching.

People who are picking up the signals of the Holy Spirit are excited people. They act like nothing's bothering them. You know why? Because they are so focused on what the Spirit is saying—not on what their situation is saying—and that makes them happy all the time. I love to be around happy people. Who doesn't?

Psalms 39:3 says, "My heart was hot within me, while I was musing the fire burned: then spake I with my tongue." The word "musing" means to meditate. Because when you begin meditating on the Word, it sets your heart on fire. There's an internal burning. That's the reason people should come around you after you've been meditating. Just to see you burn.

When you meditate, you're saturating your mind with the life and spirit of God's thoughts.

When you start thinking like God, you're going to talk like God.

Isaiah 55:8 says, "For my thoughts are not your thoughts, neither are your ways my ways, saith the Lord." When you start meditating, you will begin to think like God. His thoughts start coming in your mind and you begin to think you can do things that you know you wouldn't ordinarily think you could do.

Joshua 1:8 says, "This book of the law shall not depart out of thy mouth; but thou shalt meditate therein day and night, that thou mayest observe to do according to all that is written therein: for then thou shalt make thy way prosperous, and then thou shalt have good success."

You might be thinking, "Lord, why did you have Joshua meditate on the Word to go and take Jericho and get across the Jordan?" Because if He did not meditate on the Word, he could not have thought as he ought. In order to cross Jordan, he had to think like God. He could not think like a man. Where God was taking Joshua and the children of Israel, they had to think like Him.

When you start thinking like God, you're going to talk like God. Joshua said, "Walk around Jericho once for six days and on the seventh day walk around seven times and on the last time, just yell and your voice will bring the wall down."

Man doesn't think like that. On another occasion, Joshua was out there fighting against the Amalekites and the sun was going down and he needed more daylight to finish the fight. This man who had been meditating on the word of God day and night told the sun to stand still and the sun stood still. No normal man would even consider talking to the sun, but a man that is full of the word through meditation will begin to talk like God! To think like and get God-like results we must meditate on the His Word!

CHAPTER SIX

How To Be Led By The Holy Spirit

God wants to make our hearts sensitive to the voice of the Spirit, so that no matter how He wants to speak, or who He wants to speak through, we can be influenced by His voice.

It should be the goal of every believer to be sensitive to the Holy Spirit. We should have a drive and a passion to be sensitive to His movement. No man or woman has been one hundred percent led at all times by the Holy Spirit except Jesus. But again we are increasing our sensitivity and increasing our percentage of being in lock step with Him.

Every time we miss the Spirit, we suffer loss, suffer delay, suffer struggle. Most of our struggles in life are because we missed the Holy Spirit. And when you miss the Holy Spirit, you miss what the Father has prepared for you. We must understand this. We must have this as our drive and passion.

Romans 8:14 says, "For as many as are led by the Spirit of God, they are the sons of God." The Holy Spirit wants to take our hands and lead us to great places. To be led by the Holy Spirit is to be led into our destiny.

To be led by the Holy Spirit is to reach some places that you could've never reached by yourself. I don't know about you, but I want to carry so much glory that when people look at me, they say, "God must be in that."

The Holy Spirit will lead us into these places of pre-pared blessings. He will communicate to us what He has heard from the Father, but He'll also give us the steps, so that we can manifest those things.

So to be led by the Holy Spirit, you're going from one manifestation to another. I don't know about you, but I don't want to have years between manifestations.

What is Manifestation?

Manifestation is one of those things that already exists in the spirit realm, but it comes into our natural world where we can enjoy it. Nobody is going to enjoy things that God has prepared if they're still locked away in the spirit realm. But when they are manifested, we can see, hear, touch, taste, and smell them—we can enjoy them.

Being led by the Spirit is actually God leading us to one manifestation after another manifestation. If you're not manifesting greater things, the Holy Spirit is grieved.

Remember, it is God's will for us to partner with the Spirit to manifest supernatural things on earth. God can't get any glory if He's not seen. God is as interested in us manifesting supernatural things as we are. But we have to get to that place where we are so desperate that we say, "Lord, I don't want to do anything without the Holy Spirit. I want to make sure that I'm hearing Him, following Him, being sensitive to Him so that together we can manifest supernatural things."

However, being led by the Spirit does not cause people to be son of God. No one is one hundred percent led by the Spirit. But being sons of God qualifies us to be led by the Spirit. So never say that a person is not a son of God because the Spirit didn't lead. All of us have been in the position where we were not Spirit-led, yet we are still sons. The very presence of the Holy Spirit inside of you makes you eligible to be led into these great places.

The Holy Spirit is your partner. He wants to lead you to divinely prepared blessings. It's already done, but now the Holy Spirit wants to hold your hand and walk you into things that have already been laid out for you.

Do Not Lean On Your Own Understanding

Proverbs 3:5-6 says, "Trust in the Lord with all thine heart; and lean not unto thine own understanding. In all thy ways acknowledge him, and he shall direct thy paths."

Do you know that God has His way and we have our own understanding? And many times when we lean on our own understanding, we come up with problems.

If you're really enamored and impressed with yourself, you'll mostly lean on your own understanding. Because some of us are too smart to be led by the Holy

Ghost. A great place to trust God is when you don't trust yourself or your own decisions.

After a great manifestation, it's a dangerous time. Because many times after we get a great testimony, we somehow think we had a lot to do with it. But trusting in the Lord means to put our total person on the Lord.

The bottom line is God wants to direct us, and He has given us a partner called the Holy Spirit to lead us.

How is God going to direct your path? Psalm 37:23 says, "The steps of a good man are ordered by the Lord: and he delighteth in his way."

In the Amplified Bible it says, "The steps of a [good] man are directed and established by the Lord when He delights in his way [and He busies Himself with his every step]."

In other words, the Holy Spirit is getting busy guiding you. The Father has already been busy setting it up for you, and now the Holy Spirit is working to get you there.

How much does God really love us? In Psalms 32:8 it says, "I will instruct thee and teach thee in the way which thou shalt go: I will guide thee with mine eye."

I used to look up scriptures that had the words seek, guide, and direct in them. I would go through the whole Bible and write them all down and Psalms 32:8 was my favorite. God is saying, "I'll make sure my eye never gets off you; I'll make sure that you stay on the right path." He has set up our lives and He wants to make sure we get to see what He set up.

The bottom line is God wants to direct us, and He has given us a partner called the Holy Spirit to lead us.

Here Are 6 Ways That The Holy Spirit Leads Us:

1) Through an inner witness

Romans 8:16 says, "The Spirit itself beareth witness with our spirit, that we are the children of God."

The Holy Spirit that is housed within our spirit bears witness that we are the children of God. The Holy Spirit will give you the assurance that you are saved.

In terms of leading you, He will also give you a witness about the decisions that you make. Something will come up where you have a decision to make, and you will need to ask yourself: Is there a witness in my spirit?

If we lean on our own understanding, we can rely on logic, but is our spirit bearing witness? Many of us have gone with our logic and understanding when our spirit was saying, "No."

There are times when I want to make a decision, and the Spirit says, "No." Many times He won't tell me why. I just won't feel right about it. Many times you'll find out why later.

The primary way the Holy Spirit leads you is through an inner witness. When we let the Holy Spirit give us a witness, it keeps us from being deceived, keeps us from a lot of pain, and keeps us from a lot of wasted time and wasted ventures.

2) Through promptings

Promptings are supernatural appeals to follow a course of action. It's an urging, a supernatural appeal to do something. You'll hear believers say things like, "I was led of the Spirit."

Here's a hypothetical scenario. Say the Holy Spirit is nudging you to go to Wal-Mart, and you have no idea why. But you respond to the prompting and drive over to Walmart. You say, "I'm going to get me something while I'm over here." Then you bump into someone, and end up ministering or blessing him or her in some way, all because you obeyed the prompting of the Holy Spirit.

The Holy Spirit will prompt you to take a course of action. That's how the Spirit leads.

Romans 7:6 (AMP) says, "But now we are discharged from the Law and have terminated all intercourse with it, having died to what once restrained and held us captive. So now we serve not under [obedience to] the old code of written regulations, but [under obedience to the promptings] of the Spirit in newness [of life]."

Now, we're not led by rules, we're led by the promptings of the Holy Spirit. The Holy Spirit will prompt you to apologize. The Holy Spirit will prompt you to sow seeds.

Never ignore the promptings of the Holy Spirit because they are going to lead you into manifestation and demonstration.

Husbands, the Holy Spirit will prompt you to put your arm around your wife. I've been married for twenty-three years and let me tell you something, it isn't always lovey, lovey, lovey that causes you to do everything. The Holy Spirit will help you strike a match and bring the fire back into your marriage.

Wives, the Holy Spirit will prompt you to speak positive words to your husband instead of complaining about what he isn't doing. The Holy Spirit will prompt you to take a course of action that is going to reap great benefits.

3) Through an inner voice

Your inner voice is your spirit speaking what the Holy Spirit has received from the Father. Some people call this your conscience or intuition. A lot of times we say, "It was God." That's just fine. But I respect people who say, "It was the Holy Spirit."

Another way that the Holy Spirit deals with us is through dreams and visions. Some people ask me to interpret their dreams. I've tried, but I'm no Joseph. I have a sister who wakes up every morning and can remember her dreams. I'm like, "Come on." But now that she's saved, the Lord deals with her in her dreams.

A dream is when you're asleep, but a vision is when you're awake and you see something in the Spirit. In Acts 10:9-13 it says, "On the morrow, as they went on their journey, and drew nigh unto the city, Peter went upon the housetop to pray about the sixth hour: and he became very hungry, and would have eaten, but while they made ready, he fell into a trance, and saw heaven opened, and a certain vessel descending upon him, as it had been a great sheet knit at the four corners, and let down to the earth: Wherein were all manner of four-footed beasts of the earth, and wild beasts, and creeping things, and fowls of the air. On the morrow, as they went on their journey, and drew nigh unto the city, Peter went up upon the housetop to pray about the sixth hour: And there came a voice to him, rise, Peter; kill, and eat."

Peter said that God began to speak to him from this particular vision. Verse 19-20 says, "While Peter thought on the vision, the Spirit said unto him, 'behold, three men seek thee." He was looking on the vision and the Spirit said, "There are three men that are seeking you. Arise therefore, and get thee down, and go with them, doubting nothing: for I have sent them."

It's better to be doing something than to be waiting and not doing anything.

There was a time when I was living in Columbus, Ohio and I had worked at AT&T for a couple of years. I had a cubicle a little ways from my boss's office door. One day , I noticed that he had closed his door to take a phone call.

During that call, the Holy Spirit said, "That's Jerry from Michigan who called, and there's a job opening in Michigan and he's asking if you can take it." I just sat there. First of all, I wasn't moving to Michigan. But the Holy Ghost knew this is how He had to talk to me.

A few minutes later, my boss called me into his office and said, "I just got off the phone with Jerry and there's a job opening in Michigan and they want you to take it."

It was kind of easy for me to accept that job because the Holy Spirit had already showed me things to come.

But remember, there is a balance, which I'll go into, so that you don't start saying, "The Holy Spirit told me to cast myself into the Flint River, for He will give His angels charge over me to keep me in all my ways, lest I dash my foot against the stone."

Acts 16:6-7 says, "Now when they had gone throughout Phrygia and the region of Galatia, and were forbidden of the Holy Ghost to preach the word in Asia, after they were come to Mysia, they assayed to go into Bithynia: but the Spirit suffered them not."

They were going to these places throughout Phrygia and the region of Galatia, and were forbidden of the Holy Ghost to preach the Word in Asia.

They weren't waiting for the Holy Ghost to say, "Go." They were going and the Holy Ghost was saying, "Don't go there. Go there." The Holy Ghost began to talk to them as they moved. It's like a GPS. The guide doesn't start talking until you start driving.

Some people will say, "I'm not going to do anything because I haven't heard the Holy Ghost yet." If it's the will of God, you start doing things, and then the Holy Ghost will tell you, "No, not there. There." It's better to be doing something than to be waiting and not doing anything.

You're not going to find a job if you wait on the Holy Ghost to tell you, "Get out of the house." You're going to have to get out there and the Holy Spirit will guide you. Some people go into a mode of doing nothing. You'll ask them, "What are you waiting on?" And they'll say, "I'm waiting on the Holy Ghost." But that's not profitable in the least.

Acts 16:9-10 says, "And a vision appeared to Paul in the night; there stood a man of Macedonia, and prayed him, saying, 'Come over into Macedonia, and help us.' And after he had seen the vision, immediately we endeavored to go into Macedonia, assuredly gathering that the Lord had called us for to preach the gospel unto them."

God wouldn't let them preach in Asia, but Paul got a vision of Macedonia and he said, "I know this is what God is telling me to do." So it wasn't like they were never going to go preach in Asia, but maybe the folks in Macedonia were more hungry than those folks in Asia and there was going to be a greater response and God was saying, "The folks in Asia aren't ready." When you listen to that inner voice , you don't waste time trying to do something God never intended for you to do.

4) Through the body of Christ

Keep yourself full of the Holy Spirit through songs, hymns and spiritual songs and giving thanks to God. Ephesians 5:17 says, "Wherefore be ye not unwise, but understanding what the will of the Lord is." We all want to know what the will of the Lord is, right?

Ephesians 5:18-20 says, "And be not drunk with wine, wherein is excess; but be filled with the Spirit;

speaking to yourselves in psalms and hymns and spiritual songs, singing and making melody in your heart to the Lord; giving thanks always for all things unto God the Father in the name of our Lord Jesus Christ; submitting yourselves one to another in the fear of God."

What does submitting ourselves to one another have to do with being led by the Spirit? Well, if you can't submit to the individuals in the body of Christ, you'll never be led by the Holy Ghost because God speaks through people. He doesn't just speak to you in an inner voice, a witness, dreams or visions. He'll speak to you through gifts in the body. He'll give you a rhema, a personal word through the preached Word—a word of knowledge and a word of wisdom. He'll give you counsel.

When you really submit to the gifts in the body of Christ, you will pursue people that are more knowledgeable than you. No person can make it on their own.

But the enemy of submission is pride. A proud person can't hear anyone but himself or herself. Submitting means admitting that you don't have all the answers.

And when you really submit to the gifts in the body of Christ, you will pursue people that are more knowledgeable than you. No person can make it on their own. God gave the gifts in the body to help you make progress.

I've been married for twenty-three years, and I used to have a bad habit of not listening to my wife. She'd be talking and I'd be hearing, but I wouldn't be truly listening. But as I grew in the Lord, I realized that women equal wisdom.

The Holy Spirit uses my wife to show me the Holy Spirit's leading. For example, I wasn't going to bring Bishop Daniel Robertson to come speak to our church until a particular project was complete. I told her, "Maybe after the project because we have a lot of expenses right now, and I want to make sure we treat him right. Let's bring him in at the end of the project."

My wife said, "The best time to bring him in is right now—to pray over and release an anointing over the project" As soon as she said that, the Holy Spirit said, "You better listen to that." I said, "You're right." And it was the best decision I could've made.

Another time while I was working in Atanta, Georgia, my wife said, "We should take twenty thousand dollars out of the equity in our house and put it in the bank." I listened to my wife. And good thing I did. I got laid off my job the following week. We needed that money to live off until we got settled as Pastor in Albany, Georgia.

There are times where you have to submit to the gifts and pursue people that know more than you. That doesn't mean you have to do everything they say, but when you listen to those who are wiser than you, you just might hear the Spirit.

The Spirit can talk to you when He knows you'll listen to other people. Acts 13:2 says, "As they ministered to the Lord, and fasted, the Holy Ghost said, separate me

Barnabas and Saul for the work whereunto I have called them."

Verses 3-4 says, "And when they had fasted and prayed, and laid their hands on them, they sent them away. So they, being sent forth by the Holy Ghost, departed unto Seleucia; and from thence they sailed to Cyprus."

So even though the men spoke, it was the Holy Spirit that was leading and sending them out. So when somebody is talking to you, it may not be them leading you, it may be the Holy Spirit leading you through them.

Ask the Lord to make you sensitive to wisdom. Wisdom makes life easy. Some people are so dull that it takes the police, the ambulance, all the sirens, and a bullhorn to wake them up in the spirit. Don't be like that!

But how will you really know if it's the Holy Spirit talking to you? You'll have peace about it. Colossians 3:15 says, "And let the peace of God rule in your hearts, to which also ye are called in one body; and be ye thankful."

You are going to have to make sure that what you hear agrees with scripture.

In the Amplified Bible it says, "And let the peace (soul harmony which comes) from Christ rule (act as umpire continually) in your hearts [deciding and settling with finality all questions that arise in your minds, in that peaceful state] to which as [members of Christ's] one body you were also called [to live]. And be thankful (appreciative), giving praise to God always."

In other words, He's saying, "This peace is going to help you decide and settle the questions. Let peace be the umpire, let peace be the referee. Where there is no peace, the Holy Ghost is not involved."

But you must be warned. Make sure that you come back to the Word because the Holy Ghost speaks in Bible language. I knew a lady once who claimed that God told her to marry an already-married man. Now, that doesn't agree with the Bible at all. The Holy Ghost is not going to tell you that somebody else's man is your man. You are going to have to make sure that what you hear agrees with scripture.

5) Through confirmations

Another way that you know you're being led is by confirmation. I call them signposts. When you're going to Atlanta, there are signposts on the road saying that you're going in the right direction. If you're going up to Atlanta and you're on I75 and it says that Florida is ten miles away, you know something's wrong.

Let me tell you something, as the Holy Spirit is leading you, He will give you confirmations along the way.

Some people say, "I don't need any confirmation." That's true. You don't need confirmation, but it sure doesn't hurt to be told that you're going in the right direction. Who wants to be in the dark the whole journey?

6) Through manifestations

One of the greatest ways that you know the Holy Spirit is leading you is through manifestations. It just floors me when people say, "The Holy Ghost said this or that," yet you see no manifestation in their life.

Another word for manifestation is results. That's how you know for a fact that the Holy Spirit led you. There's nothing wrong with receiving a sign to let you know that you're in the right place.

God knows where our maturity level is and He'll deal with us at that level. He has set up some great things, but we can only receive those great things if we allow the Holy Spirit to take us by the hand and lead us.

CHAPTER SEVEN

Following The Spirit, Overcoming The Flesh

I want to make a link between overcoming the flesh and following the Spirit. I want to show you how following the Spirit and being led by the Spirit is the key to overcoming the flesh. Most of the time when we've heard about overcoming the flesh, it's always been through self-effort—"I've got to fast and pray—mortify the deeds of the flesh—I've got to put it down." I'm going to show you how the key to overcoming the flesh is following the Spirit. I know a lot of people have their own theology, "Now wait a minute Pastor, you still have to fast and pray." I didn't say you didn't have to fast and pray, but a lot of people fast and pray and are still overcome by the flesh. We've got a lot of fasting and praying folks overcome by the flesh. Some of them were fasting when the flesh got them.

Let's talk about this thing called the flesh and how we can overcome it. When you were born again, the old nature died, and the Holy Spirit placed you into the body of Christ, where you now have the power to overcome the flesh.

Romans 6:6 says, "Knowing this, that our old man is crucified with him, that the body of sin might be destroyed, that henceforth we should not serve sin."

The Holy Spirit has been with you ever since you were saved. And He will never leave you nor forsake you. The Bible says the old man died the moment you were planted with Christ.

The Sin Nature Died but the Flesh Remained

The old man left a residue called the body of sin and that is what we will call the flesh. When the old man was living before salvation, he programmed us to think a certain way. Some people have quick tempers. Some people don't trust God. Some people lust. Some people steal. Some people stretch the truth.

The old man programmed sinful ways into our mind. And even after we are saved, the programming remains. That's called the flesh. So even though you have been born again, you can still be operating in the old way.

The Holy Spirit didn't teach you to get drunk or to behave in sexually inappropriate ways. Sin existed long before Christ came to earth.

Some people still trip up in these certain areas after they're saved, simply because the flesh is still there and their mind has not been renewed by the Word of God.

But until you start thinking a different way, you'll still be doing the old things. Many churches have said,

"When you get saved, you are in a war with the flesh." Some of us have been fighting the flesh for twenty years and we've been losing every day. That's because we don't know how to fight. Have you ever sworn to God you're not going to do something and then you go ahead and do it again? That's because you're relying on your own self-effort and willpower rather than the power of the Holy Spirit.

You Can't Drive In Two Different Directions At The Same Time

The fight between the flesh and the Spirit is a real fight. Galatians 5:17 says, "For the flesh lusteth against the Spirit, and the Spirit against the flesh: and these are contrary the one to the other: so that ye cannot do the things that ye would." Notice that the flesh lusteth against the Spirit and the Spirit lusteth against the flesh. The flesh and the Spirit are contrary to one to another.

Now this word lusteth is not sexual in nature. The word "lust" is not always used in terms of sexual sin. For instance, if the Spirit is lusting after the flesh, it certainly is not sexual. But it does mean strong desire. Galatians 5:17 essentially means that the flesh has strong desires and the Spirit has strong desires. And the Spirit's desires are opposite of the flesh's desires.

You cannot follow the Spirit and the flesh at the same time because their desires are contrary—one is going one way and the other is going another way. And you cannot go in two directions at the same time. You cannot indulge in the Spirit and the flesh at the same time. It's impossible. You can't be in two cars at the same time. No, you're going to be in one car or the other—Spirit car or flesh car. Pretty straightforward isn't it?

Romans 8:5 says, "For they that are after the flesh do mind the things of the flesh; but they that are after the Spirit the things of the Spirit."

You cannot mind the Spirit and be minding the flesh at the same time. It's impossible! I can't even think two different thoughts at the same time. I'm either going to mind the flesh or I'm going to mind the Spirit. I can't mind them both. To mind or follow one of them is to cut the other one off. This is where you win the fight against the flesh – you simply follow the leading of the Spirit. As you are led by the Spirit, its impossible to fulfill the lust of the flesh. That's pretty simple.

God Has Given Us A Choice

The Holy Ghost is a gentleman. He's not going to sit there and beat you down. He's going to say, "Come with me." You're either going to follow Him or you're going to follow the flesh. And we've all picked up the signal of the Holy Spirit at one point in time and turned Him down. It didn't turn out really well, did it? You can either choose peace and life or misery and death.

Romans 8:6 says, "For to be carnally minded is death; but to be spiritually minded is life and peace."

In the Amplified Bible, this particular verse says, "Now the mind of the flesh [which is sense and reason without the Holy Spirit] is death [death that comprises all the miseries arising from sin, both here and hereafter].

But the mind of the [Holy] Spirit is life and [soul] peace [both now and forever]."

So, whichever way you're leaning will determine your quality of life. What is your quality of life right now? Is it misery after misery after misery? God didn't set that up and neither did the devil. The verse says you have two options: either you're going to be spiritually minded or you're going to be carnally minded.

When you follow the flesh, it's going to be death— death in relationships, death in your finances, death in your parenting, death with your children. It doesn't mean literal death. Just dead living.

But if you follow after the Spirit, there will be life in every area. People will look at you and say, "It seems like they've got it all together." Now hear me, no one has it all together, but when you're following the Spirit, it means you're spiritually minded. And when you are spiritually minded, life runs smoother. You choose your own quality of life. What way will you choose?

The Flesh Hates God's Plans

The Holy Spirit is trying to lead us to God's plans, but our carnal minds are hostile.

Romans 8:7-8 says, "Because the carnal mind is enmity against God: for it is not subject to the law of God, neither indeed can it be. So then they that are in the flesh cannot please God."

The word "enmity" means hostile or in total opposition. So the carnal mind is in total opposition to the plans of God for your life.

The Holy Spirit is trying to lead you into places where God can get ultimate glory, so that when you get there you'll see the manifestation of the glory of God. And His glory will bring you blessing. What a beautiful truth.

Finishing the Works of the Flesh

Rejecting the flesh is not an act of your will. It is an act of the Spirit. Romans 8:13 says, "For if ye live after the flesh, ye shall die: but if ye through the Spirit do mortify the deeds of the body, ye shall live."

Galatians 5:16 says, "This I say then, Walk in the Spirit, and ye shall not fulfill the lust of the flesh." This word "walk" in the Greek means how you are carrying yourself. So if you follow the Spirit, you cannot and will not fulfill the lust of the flesh. That word "fulfill" in the Greek means teleo. It's the same word that Jesus used at Calvary when He said, "It is finished."

When the Spirit leads you, the flesh will not finish. That does not mean that the flesh won't try its best to pull you down. It just means that it will never finish what it wants you to finish. It may start something, but when you walk in the light of the Spirit, the flesh loses its power.

Trying to kill the flesh is like trying to drive darkness out of a room before the light shows up. It's foolish. You don't have to deal with the darkness on your own. Just flip on the light. As soon as you flip on the light, the darkness is gone.

When you walk in the light of the Spirit, the flesh has no power. You won't have to fight it off. Following the Holy Spirit will cut it off!

At one time, we were all living solely in the flesh. But now that we know the importance of following the Spirit, the flesh has no chance.

CHAPTER EIGHT

Manifesting Things On Earth

The Holy Spirit has orders from the Father to make supernatural things happen on earth, and He's looking for someone who will cooperate with Him.

1 Corinthians 2:9-12 says, "But as it is written, Eye hath not seen, nor ear heard, neither have entered into the heart of man, the things which God hath prepared for them that love him. But God hath revealed them unto us by his Spirit: for the Spirit searcheth all things, yea, the deep things of God. For what man knoweth the things of a man, save the spirit of man which is in him? Even so the things of God knoweth no man, but the Spirit of God. Now we have received, not the spirit of the world, but the spirit which is of God; that we might know the things that are freely given to us of God."

Notice the word "things." I want to talk about manifesting things on the earth. If the Father has prepared some things for us—He does not intend for those things to stay lodged in the spirit realm. If someone left an inheritance, they intended for you to access it when you need it. God does not need the blessings and the things that He has prepared for you in heavenly places. He prepares them there, but His intention is for those things to get to us in the natural realm.

The Holy Spirit is the note-taker in Heaven; He's seen what the Father has prepared.

I don't know about anybody else, but I want my things. Anybody want their things? You need those things. Every thing that fails to be manifest in your life— you struggle because you never get them. Whatever fails to get to you from the spirit realm—causes you to struggle because it never got to you. Our struggle in the natural realm is because things have not been manifested from the spiritual realm and God has given us a supernatural partner to make things manifest.

It's right there in the text, it says, "Eye hath not seen, nor ear heard, neither have entered into the heart of man, the "things" which God hath prepared for them that love him. But God hath revealed them…" What's the them? "Things"! God has revealed the things unto us by the Holy Spirit. For the Holy Spirit searcheth all things, yea, the deep things of God. Again, the Holy Spirit is the note-taker in Heaven; He's seen what the Father has prepared. Whatever He hears that is what He speaks, according to St. John 16:13. Whatever He hears He speaks. He shows us things to come. God has a plan, He has these things, He speaks it to the Holy Spirit, and then the Holy Spirit reveals those things to us. He'll tell you, "This is what the Father has prepared for you." You don't have them in your hand, and you'll never get them in your hand until you first have a conviction in your spirit that they're real. I don't see it but I know it's real and I know it exists. It does not exist in my hand, but it exists because the Father has prepared it. Now the Holy Spirit has revealed it unto me and He's going to assist me so I can get my things and the things the Father wants me to manifest on earth.

Your money, your healing, your new heart, your new kidney, better blood, it exists, and the Father has prepared it.

Notice it says in verse 12, "Now we have received, not the spirit of the world, but the spirit which is of God; that we might know the things that are freely given to us of God." These things don't even cost you anything. The Bible says right there, "they are freely given..." Freely given, now we know we like free. Now, your things are not my things and my things are not your things, but you have some things and I have some things. I'm getting my things, and hopefully you get your things.

There are two different realms—there's the spirit realm and the natural realm. The realm of the spirit is not in some far distant country, it's not way out in the heavenlies—the spirit realm is in you. Ephesians 1:3 says, God has already blessed you with every spiritual blessing in heavenly places in Christ Jesus. If Jesus is in you, and He is, the spirit realm that houses your blessings is in you too! You did not originate these "things" in the spirit realm. No, no, no, the Father originated them. You cannot see it, hear it, touch it, taste it, and smell it. Your senses won't be satisfied with the spirit realm, the sixth sense, called faith is what picks up what's in the spirit realm.

So there is an unseen realm called the spiritual realm. Then there is a physical realm where we live, where we enjoy our world. There is nothing wrong with the senses because you need the senses to enjoy this natural world.

God does His work in the spirit realm. He provides your blessings in the spirit realm. God does not hurl your miracle down to earth—He puts it in the spirit realm. All of your things, they currently exist, right now, but they exist in the spirit realm. They currently exist, they exist right now. You may not be able to see it but it's already there. You don't see all your money in the bank right now, but that doesn't mean it's not there.

Your money, your healing, your new heart, your new kidney, better blood, it exists, and the Father has prepared it. It's in another realm.

Then the Father gives us the Holy Spirit, and the Holy Spirit comes and says, "I heard something from the Father. I was in the meeting and I heard what the Father said and He wants me to come down here to tell you." He didn't have to zip down and tell you—the Holy Spirit exists now in your born again spirit. He knows the deep things, because He searches the deep things of God. He went into the areas of the things that the Father has prepared for you; found them out; heard about it; and then came and said, "Let me tell you what's going on here, in a realm that you can't see." Isn't that powerful?

We have this partner now to help us manifest, to help us bring the things out of the unseen realm into the seen.

Then the Father gave us a partner to make it happen or to manifest the "things". The Holy Spirit—He's a paraklétos. A paraklétos is one that comes along side to aid. In other words, He is with us twenty-four seven. He said He would never leave us, nor forsake us. That means whatever decisions we must make; we have a partner and that we can say, "What do you think about it?" He leads us, He guides us. He shows us where these prepared things are.

There is this word called manifestation. To manifest—it means to make known to the senses—readily perceived by the senses ... especially the sight. To manifest is to make know to the senses—I didn't see it, but when it was manifested I can see it, I can touch it, and I can enjoy it. The word manifest, it implies it was already there.

Nothing is manifest that did not already exist before it was manifest. When my wife and I were having problems having children, our pastor prophesied over us that she would get pregnant and have this child and my wife began to believe by faith. She began to do things as if the baby was already there...buying onesies and stuff. Going and just buying stuff—getting the room together. In her mind it was a done deal—he existed. So we have this partner now to help us manifest, to help us bring the things out of the unseen realm into the seen.

The Holy Spirit—He is the most important person on earth right now. He has orders from the Father to make some supernatural things happen on earth. He has orders to make earth look like Heaven. And then He has some subjects called saints—folks like Scott Sanders, and the Father says, "Partner with Sanders to make some supernatural things happen. Partner with whoever will cooperate and make some supernatural things happen on earth, make earth look like Heaven." He's looking for someone who will cooperate with Him. Is it you? Will you cooperate with the Holy Spirit? He looked at me and said, "Would you work with me to make some things happen? Would you work with me?" He's looking for someone who will be more sympathetic to His will than just sensitive to their own world—own life. When you want to cooperate with the Holy Spirit you've got to lose yourself. You've got set down your agenda. You've got to lay down your life and say, "Holy Spirit, I'm going your way." The great thing is when you go the Holy Spirit's way—that's when you're really going to have real fulfillment. You can't have it both ways. You can't have your life and cooperate with the Holy Spirit. See for a long time in my ministry, I didn't understand. I'd been asking the Holy Ghost to breathe on what I did. But now I'm saying, "Lord, help me to do what you're breathing on." Oh Lord, don't just bless my plans, helps me to be doing your plans.

See once we start doing His will there's already provision there, power there, everything you need because it's His thing not yours. How can you ever have shortage when you're doing His will? How can you ever run out when it's all about Him and not about you? Are you saying the kingdom won't back you up when all you're doing is focusing on the will of the kingdom. God said to me, "Do what I tell you to do and money will never be an issue." He didn't just say, "Be a pastor. Do what I tell you to do and money will never be an issue." Because God is going to take care of whoever is pushing His product.

Partner With The Holy Spirit To Do Supernatural Things

God intended for our spirit and the Holy Spirit to get together and cause supernatural things to happen on earth. Jesus said in St. John 14:12, "Verily, verily, I say unto you, He that believeth on me, the works that I do shall he do also; and greater works than these shall he do; because I go unto my Father." Jesus said, "When I get back to my Father, I'm going to send the Holy Ghost". The Holy Ghost is going to come down and work with us—work with our spirit, so we can do the same thing Jesus did and greater works—not greater in quality but greater in quantity because there are more of us.

God has intended for our spirit and the Holy Spirit to work together to make some things happen, like create. Listen, we've been made in the image of God. What does that mean? God has given us faith—that's what He had when he created the heavens and the earth. God has given us a mouth to create, to speak. We cause things to happen on earth and if we don't get involved, even though God has an intention for something to happen down here, it can never happen because He has to use a man or a woman—He must use a human being so that things that He has intended from Heaven, can manifest on earth. He cannot do it and will not do it by Himself. Since creation, He's never done anything on earth by himself. God just couldn't come and redeem mankind. No, He had to use a man. He has to work through a man. Once He created Adam, God couldn't even name the animals—man had to do everything through the leading and empowerment of God. So we've been partnering with God for years—making things happen on earth. Now is not the time for us to get saved and relax and say, "I'm on my way to Heaven and I'm so glad." God wants to use us. The great thing about God using us is that when He uses us, He benefits those that He uses.

Beware of a Dull Soul

Remember that man is a triconomy: spirit, soul, and body. The issue really is this: the Holy Spirit cannot operate through a dull soul and a contrary body. The Holy Spirit speaks to your spirit, your spirit begins to speak to your soul, but the Holy Spirit cannot operate when your soul is dull. It's critical that we have our mind renewed by the Word of God. The more we receive the Word, our mind begins to agree with our spirit. And the Word of God is reprogramming the mind and the mind now is leaning toward the spirit.

There can't be manifestation without all three parts of man being involved. If the spirit is working but the mind isn't working, there's no manifestation. If the mind is imperceptive and dull, the body will not act in faith and prepare for what the mind believes.

The soul, the mind is now minding the spirit and not minding the flesh/the body. But watch this, if the mind is dull and imperceptive—even though it's hearing spiritual things, it cannot perceive them. The more the Word changes our thinking, the more the Holy Spirit can begin to flow. Now watch this, once the Holy Spirit begins to flow and our mind begins to pick up the signals, we become perceptive—that's called revelation. And now, that same word begins to affect what we see and sense, and now we're telling the body, "It's time to do some things." Now the body is not contrary, because the mind is saying, "You're not in control—I'm in control. I'm under new management, the leading of my spirit. Now we're going to take some steps to manifest some supernatural things."

There can't be manifestation without all three parts of man being involved. If the spirit is working but the mind isn't working, there's no manifestation. If the mind is imperceptive and dull, the body will not act in faith and prepare for what the mind believes. And it's very important to understand that there is no graduation in the area of manifestation—because after one manifestation, there's another one that God wants to do and you've got to get your mind and body involved with your spirit.

Something You Must Understand

There is a threefold government in Heaven and a threefold government in earth. The threefold government in Heaven is called the Father, the Son, and the Holy Ghost. The threefold government in earth is the spirit, the soul, and the body. Heaven gets together and wants to do some things, the Father, the Son, and the Holy Spirit, being one, they get together and they begin to plan some things for earth. Now on earth, there is a threefold government: spirit, soul, body, one person. In Psalms 115:15-16 it makes it very clear about these governments when it says, "Ye are blessed of the Lord which made heaven and earth. The heaven, even the heavens, are the Lord's: but the earth hath he given to the children of men."

So Heaven is God's domain, where He governs. Earth is man's domain where we govern. And if anything is going to happen on earth, then The Lord has to work with man whom He's given authority over earth in order for those things to appear or to manifest. It is critical that you understand this because if you don't understand this, you don't even understand the role your spirit, soul and body play in manifesting supernatural things on earth.

You can't get upset with the service provider when you haven't done your part.

The government in Heaven prepares it and the government on earth manifests it. If things don't happen in my life, I can't blame God. If your cellphone stops working and you haven't paid the bill, you can't blame the service provider. I recently took a phone back to Verizon. It was dark and inoperable—I plug it in the outlet and there was nothing but black. I said to myself, "My God, I just got a replacement phone." I took it down to the local store and I wasn't indignant but I was like, "My goodness, I just got this phone." And the gentleman said, "Do you have your power adapter." I said, "No, I don't have my power adapter, I figured you guys would have some power somewhere." They went and got some power, plugged it up, and he said, "Oh yeah, the power is on." I said, "No sir, it's black." He said, "yes it's black but if you look real close there is a little flicker of light, it's just that you had gone to total zero power and you didn't know it."

I was getting upset with them but it wasn't their issue—it was mine. You can't get upset with the service provider when you haven't done your part. And a lot of us are blaming God for things, but we—our spirit, soul, and body—have not cooperated with the Holy Spirit to make things happen and we're frustrated. I'm not trying to blame you, but I am trying to say you have something to do with your own manifestation. Government in Heaven prepared it, government on earth manifests it. If it's going to happen, you must be involved.

The Supernatural System of God

God made us to manifest invisible things on earth. The way God created you, He created you so that you could bring invisible things into a visible world. The things He put on you and in you were to make sure that you can make invisible things appear. He created mankind with what's called the infrastructure to produce invisible things—the spirit, the soul, and the body. Our spirit, soul and body is a manifesting system. If the systems of this world can't help you, you have a supernatural system that God created to produce supernatural things!

All of us—not just one or a few of us—have a spirit. In fact we are spirit. The real you is spirit. We were spirit before we were ever a body. We always existed in spirit form, you say, "Pastor, we didn't always exist." Well the Bible says, "God choose you in Him before the foundation of the world." How could He chose you if you did not exist? You did exist—in spirit form. That's the real you. You are spirit that is housed within a body that has a soul. God put everything in us so that we could cooperate with the Holy Spirit to manifest supernatural things, invisible things. Things that don't yet exist in the natural, but they exist in the spirit. He gave you a spirit to pick up what the Holy Spirit was saying. He gave you a spirit to house and become the temple of the Holy Spirit. The Holy Spirit dwells on the inside of your spirit. In fact, your spirit and the Holy Spirit are so intertwined that when God looks at you He sees the Spirit of Christ. The Bible says in 1 Corinthians 6:17, "But he that is joined unto the Lord is one spirit." So when the Holy Spirit is in your spirit, God sees it as one spirit. The same recreated spirit, the same spirit as Jesus. The same potential as Jesus! Now our spirit can pick up these signals from the Holy Spirit. Then our spirit begins to speak to our minds, that's called revelation. God created us to manifest some supernatural works. Ephesians 2:10 says, "For we are his workmanship, created in Christ Jesus unto good works, which God hath before ordained that we should walk in them." In other words, God has ordained for us to operate and manifest some works. He created us so that we could do some works that He ordained for us. He placed the Holy Spirit within us, the Holy Spirit is speaking to our spirit, and our spirit is speaking to our mind.

When we see clearly, we begin to act on what we believe. First we see it. Then we start taking steps.

When my mind begins to pick up what my spirit is saying I begin to see, not with my natural eyes, I begin to see on the inside. That is called imagination. You begin to project something in your future that's not in your present. And you begin to set your life up around what you see. It's not yet gotten to faith, but faith starts off as imagination. You've been able to see yourself doing something that you're not doing right now. Imagination is also called hope or expectation or a positive expectation of good. Whatever I can internally see, I can have. If I can hold it in my mind, it's only a matter of time before I'm holding it in my hand.

Years ago, I used to do the long-jump. I used to visualize the whole thing in my mind. I'd say to myself, "I'm running down the runway, I'm picking up speed, I'm hitting that penultimate stride and—BOOM. I hit that board—POW. I'm running, I'm running, and I'm running!"

As soon as I took off, I acted out the moves that I saw in my mind. When I could see it clearly, I could be it clearly.

And when we see clearly, we begin to act on what we believe. First we see it. Then we start taking steps. We can't take steps without our body and we can't have faith without action. When the woman with the issue of blood heard about Jesus, she began to say, "If I touch the hem of His garment, I'll be made whole." She began to see this in her mind, and then she began to say it out of her mouth. She got up and she got into the press, she began to act, that's called faith. Because faith has feet, and faith has a mouth.

This is how manifesting invisible things on earth works: The spirit picks up the message, the spirit relays the message to the mind, the mind begins to imagine, and then it begins to push the body so much that the body begins to act in faith.

The devil is after your mind and he's definitely after your mouth. If he can shut you up from saying, "This is going to happen," then he will.

When you really begin to imagine something, you're not scared. You'll go out in a battle like David and say, "Goliath listen, I'm about to take your sword and cut off your head." Everything that David said, he did. Whatever you believe, you're going to begin to speak.

The devil is after your mind and he's definitely after your mouth. If he can shut you up from saying, "This is going to happen," then he will. Because he knows if he shuts up your mouth, he shuts up your manifestation.

Right now, you have everything you'll ever need to manifest supernatural things. And the greatest thing you have is the Holy Spirit.

Whenever the devil knows that you're on to something great, he'll throw some frustration in your life to shut you up. But when it doesn't look like it's going to happen, that's when you better start speaking even more.

You better wake up in the morning and say, "Lord, let me be a part of what you're doing. Not what I'm doing. Help me to cooperate with you because I know there are things you want to manifest on earth."

We have a partner who knows all things. He knows what the Father has prepared for us and He's going to work with us, if only we cooperate with Him.

Can you imagine what your life will look like when you let the Holy Spirit have His way? I really believe that if we could zero in on the power of the Holy Spirit, nothing could stop us.

If we could zero in on the power of the Holy Spirit, nothing could stop us.

About The Author

Pastor Scott T. Sanders is the pastor and founder of Rhema International Ministries, Inc. He founded the ministry in 2003 and the Lord made it very clear that he is a chosen vessel for this generation. Pastor Sanders has been married for 23 years to Cynthia R. Sanders and is the father to their two sons, Scott II (Ty) and Justin.

Rhema International Ministries has reached several milestones under Pastor Sanders' leadership. In 2005 the church purchased 9.5 acres and in 2009 the first sanctuary was erected. In 2010, the church purchased an additional 12 acres of land adjacent to the church. In 2012, the church cancelled the entire mortgage and land debt and is currently "Debt Free."

Pastor Sanders has many accomplishments in corporate and religious environments. As a corporate leader for 10 years he held managerial positions within the telecommunications industry having local, regional and international operations responsibilities.

Pastor Sanders is a dynamic preacher and teacher who proclaims the almost-too-good-to-be-true news of the Gospel. His messages and teaching series' are full of revelation and are geared to break religious traditions and transform minds so that the body of Christ can manifest God's glory. Pastor Sanders is also the founder and president of the STS School of Discipleship, a three-course training specializing in teaching foundational truths to leaders, ministers and laymen, giving them a stronger foundation for ministry.

Pastor Sanders received his Masters Certificate in Project Management from George Washington University. He also received his Bachelors and Masters of Science Degrees from Ball State University. His personal mission statement reads: *My intention in life is to use my preaching, teaching and leadership gifts to win lost souls to Christ and to inspire and equip individuals to fulfill their life's calling.*

Phone: 1-229-434-9673
Web: freshrhema.org, scottsandersministries.org

About SermonToBook.Com

SermonToBook.com began with a simple belief: that sermons should be touching lives, *not* collecting dust. That's why we turn sermons into high-quality books that are accessible to people all over the globe.

Turning your sermon or sermon series into a book exposes more people to God's Word, better equips you for counseling, accelerates future sermon prep, adds credibility to your ministry, and even helps make ends meet during tight times.

John 21:25 tells us that the world itself couldn't contain the books that would be written about the work of Jesus Christ. Our mission is to try anyway. Because, in Heaven, there will no longer be a need for sermons or books. Our time is now.

If God so leads you, we'd love to work with you on your sermon or sermon series.

Visit www.sermontobook.com to learn more.

YOUR PROBLEMS
HAVE PURPOSE
Purpose
UNDERSTANDING GOD'S PLAN
FOR YOUR LIFE
STEVE BOZEMAN

All Problems in your past, present and future have a Purpose to fulfill in your life! The problems you are dealing with are leaving you frustrated, depressed and feeling like God has abandoned you. You've been praying for relief and you've even tried to borrow relief, but nothing is working. You constantly question, "Why all of these problems, God?"

Your Problems Have Purpose is an engaging book, full of practical life-application principles including:

- Discovering who you are in Christ
- Growing in God's purpose for you
- Learning how to overcome the fact that brokenness hurts
- Submitting to God's will for your life and living successfully

Additionally you'll learn…

- Exactly how God uses your problems to develop your purpose
- Why God uses problems to protect you from yourself
- What your purpose cost God

Discover how important your problems are to God's purposeful plan for your life, and how the RIGHT perspective makes all the difference!

Purchase today on Amazon.com!

SPENDING
TIME WITH
GOD

GOD'S DAILY PRESENCE FULFILLS YOUR GREATEST PURPOSE

JAMES THOMAS

Spending time with God is one of the greatest privileges you have in life. Greater than your public worship, greater than your spiritual gifts, greater than preaching and teaching the gospel. When you commit yourself to spending time with your Heavenly Father on a daily basis, it will change your life. Period.

God wants to spend time with you, not because He's lonely, but because you so desperately need His daily presence in order to fulfill your greatest purpose.

In *Spending Time With God*, you'll learn super practical ways to draw near to your Heavenly Father and experience life-changing transformation as He draws near to you. For starters, you'll discover:

• 4 disciplines that motivate and inspire spending time with God

• The incredible impact of spending time with God

• Required elements for spending time with God

• The power of prayer and praise while spending time with God

Prepare yourself for the spectacular. Because when you experience God's daily presence, He fulfills your greatest purpose.

Purchase today on Amazon.com!